Simplicity

Simplicity

KINGDOM LIVING THROUGH THE EYES OF A CHILD

BETTY MALZ

Chosen Books

A Division of Baker Book House Co
Grand Rapids, Michigan 49516

Published by Chosen Books
a division of Baker Book House Company
P.O. Box 6287, Grand Rapids, MI 49516-6287

Printed in the United States of America

Library of Congress Cataloging-in-Publication Data

Malz, Betty.
   Simplicity : kingdom living through the eyes of a child / Betty Malz.
      p. cm.
   Includes bibliographical references.
   ISBN 0-8007-9240-8 (cloth)
   1. Christian life. 2. Simplicity—Religious aspects—Christianity.
   3. Children—Religious life. I. Title.
   BV4501.2.M3348 1996
   248.4—dc20

                                     95-43028

This book is dedicated to Diane Cunningham, mother of tiny twin daughters and wife of Benny Cunningham. She does not promote her position, does not advertise, specialize, publicize or glamorize. She simply "does it" with enthusiasm and efficiency. She and Pastor Benny are partners for a purpose.

Contents

Preface

uddenly awakened from a sound sleep by a *thud*, I sat straight up in bed. Looking out the bedroom window, I saw a car speeding away from our driveway. At daybreak, I went downstairs and found the source of that thud: the biggest Sunday edition of the St. Petersburg *Times* I had ever seen.

Heaving the newspaper up the sixteen steps to our little four-room stilt house, I put it on the scales in our kitchen. It was seven and a half pounds of bad news: O. J. Simpson, the Oklahoma City bombing, restlessness in the Middle East.

Then, just inches away on the breakfast bar, I saw it—a half pound of cure—my New Testament.

I opened it to Revelation 12:12 and understood why we have all the bad news: "The devil has come down to you, having great wrath, because he knows that he has a short time."

But tucked inside my Testament as a book marker was a photo of our youngest child, April, at about three years old. I remembered my grandmother's insistence that we adults could learn simplicity and survival from children if we would quit thinking like adults. This, I realized, was the key to survival in a bad-news world: becoming like a child, thinking like a child, simply trusting like a child. Jesus said it point-blank: "Unless you are converted [change] and become as little children, you will by no means enter the kingdom of heaven" (Matthew 18:3).

Art Linkletter wrote a book entitled *Kids Say the Darndest Things*. My husband, Carl, and I bought editions one and two of Linkletter's televised interviews with children and found them delightfully entertaining. Reading the book and seeing the little ones' fresh, honest responses, I became more impressed with the need for a book on simplicity based on the wisdom and characteristics of children. Still, are we, as my grandmother also insisted, too smart to understand?

Go to the cemetery. Look at the gravestones. Under each name you will see the date of birth and the date of death. Between the two dates is a dash. From the womb to the tomb—a mad dash—rush—hurry—and die.

God has a better plan: He wants us to start over like children. Rather than being troubled about many things, we must realize that we do not need to know how to fly: We live with the Pilot. We do not need formulas: We have the Father.

And the Father wants us to become childlike. This does not mean childish. He does not require us to shift our brains into neutral, but to live in the Spirit, walk in the Spirit, be led by the Spirit, traveling in overdrive all the while.

How did I come to these simple solutions to very complex questions? Good things are expensive. I am not just an idle dreamer, but have waded through adversities—no, I have rushed, jetted wearily through schedules, climbing mountains, trying to lift others.

At 3:33 one morning my pillow was wet from crying. My sheets were wound and tied like a pretzel. I had been rolling and tossing from the anxiety of the past two years of rushing complexity, confusion, depression, heartache, disappointment, compassion fatigue, overwork, misunderstanding, criticism, hurt and self-pity.

Turning fretfully I cried out Elizabeth Akers Allen's words, learned so long ago, "Backward, turn backward, O time, in your flight, make me a child again, just for tonight!"

I recalled my rich family heritage with its deep roots of faith, and longed for the security and simplicity of those childhood years when we lived in a small Hoosier town in western Indiana. All my relatives lived within a mile or two of each other, supporting, helping, caring, praying, giving and loving. On Sunday morning and on Sunday and Wednesday nights I could look around our humble church and see my great-grandmother, Mom and Dad Perky (my paternal grandparents) and Mom and Dad Burns (my maternal grandparents). I saw all my aunts and uncles and all of their children following after Christ, serving God, worshiping together, bound by blood ties, bound by God, our faith and the church.

Could any of this simple bliss be recaptured now, today? I wondered. I believe it can. Millions of other people yearn for simplicity and meaning in their lives.

This is my prayer for you, my reader: "May God, by the Holy Spirit, my prompter, the One called alongside, help us learn from the children, sort out our priorities, simplify and then rely on Him and Him alone for the keys to vibrant, valiant living. From where You sit, You have all the answers. Amen."

In chapter 1 we will explore the biblical basis for simplicity, and look at three childlike practices many adults need to relearn.

Acknowledgments

> "I could not, would not, want to live in a world without children."
>
> Karen Siddle

I was Karen Siddle's housemother in college. We had lost track of each other for eighteen years; then she came on staff as associate pastor at the church in Dunedin, Florida, where my husband, Carl, pastored. A children's pastor, youth pastor and teacher of children from kindergarten to grade twelve, she has also served as chaplain for children who were terminally ill in Orlando. Karen speaks and conducts women's retreats on communication, building bridges, prayer and relationships.

Many of the practical parables from babes and very young children that appear in this book have come out of Karen's family and teaching experiences.

ONE

Simplicity

A Little Child Shall Lead Them

Simplicity is probably the most complicated of accomplishments. In a society in which we are blessed with more leisure time than any human beings in history, why do we feel frazzled with to-do lists, agendas, schedules and details? In a world inundated with gadgets designed to make our lives easier, why are so many of us finding a simpler life elusive?

Some time ago, a young woman friend drove me to the Tampa airport to catch a flight to Denver. The early morning traffic on the Gulf Coast of Florida was a zoo. I had no idea there were so many school buses on the West Coast. I thought this was a retirement state! And apparently every Canadian had decided to stay two more days before heading home. One local resident's bumper sticker read, "Teach a Yankee to Drive—Head His Car North!"

Please do not misunderstand me. Everyone I know used to be somebody else, from somewhere else, and I am a transplanted Yankee myself. Besides, I work part-time at

Tissy's Boutique in Palm Harbor, and we love those "snow-birds" who appreciate the pretty things we have for sale.

But our highway confusion threatened to make me miss my flight, and my young friend was clearly agitated. She sat tense, with furrowed brow, gripping the steering wheel, tears brimming in her soft brown eyes as she fought traffic and raced with the clock, her two babies strapped into their car seats in the back of her small van. Suddenly she burst out, "The media demands that I be informed; television suggests I must be thin; Hollywood expects me to be beautiful; the pastor wants me good; my husband wants me passionate; my kids want me home, but the economy makes it necessary for me to work and make money. Stop the world, I want to get off! I feel like giving up. I don't need another challenge, don't want another mountain to climb. What I really long for is *simplicity;* time to screw my head on straight; to put both feet on the ground at the same time—on level ground. I just want to survive!"

It was so typical of our busy lives that I had no chance that day to respond to her plea, to remind her that Jesus longs for us to experience the very simplicity she was craving. The sheriff directed traffic around a school bus that had broken down on the Courtney Campbell Causeway, and my driver swerved into the airport's departure lane. Before she had come to a complete stop, I opened the door and rushed up the escalator, glad I had only carry-on baggage. Out of breath from running, I arrived at the jetway door just as the gate attendant closed it. With a pitiful look, I bowed my head and made praying hands. She let me on.

People looked daggers at me as I hurried down the aisle to my seat. Someone else was already in it, so I slumped into a vacant one. There was no room in the overhead compartment, so I crammed my briefcase and carry-on underfoot, further crowding my weary, 5 foot 12 inch body for the three-and-a-half hour flight to Denver.

I hate to dress up and travel. I would rather be home, barefoot, just writing. I never cry (in fact, I laugh too much), but by now I was wrung out, near tears. I reached into my briefcase, took out a "Do not disturb" sign from a motel and hung it on the front center button of my pelican blouse. Closing my eyes, I saw and heard all over again my doctor's recent warning: "Betty, you've got to avoid stress."

"Doctor," I had explained, "I am avoiding stress. But you must talk to stress and tell it to avoid me. I didn't ask for a root canal with complications, costing me $1,300. I didn't ask that kid driving his mother's Jimmy without permission to cross a double yellow line and cram the front of my old 1962 MG while I sat innocently waiting for the light to change. I didn't plan for my house to be robbed, and my wedding ring, among other things, to be stolen at noon last Tuesday while I was at Clearwater Beach. I didn't want to break my foot when I crammed it into the railing of the sundeck to keep my kitten from escaping to the traffic below. I'm suffering stressure and press, which is more fatal than pressure and stress."

I felt better after I awakened from a twenty-minute power nap, but that was not going to remedy my complex life. Reaching into the seat pocket in front of me, I pulled out a USAir flight magazine to read yet another article about stress and technology. "Living these days is like a grammar lesson—the past is perfect, but the present is tense," commented the author, Dr. Bruce Baldwin.

I agree. Little problems invade every day. I am frustrated and blow up constantly. Even when I am relaxing, I have trouble doing just one thing at a time. Work and homemaking have become complicated beyond belief. As adults we must deal with massive amounts of new information: helping children with complex homework; using calculators; learning to operate home computers, VCRs and microwave ovens; and always coping with new and fluctuating tax laws.

Maybe you remember when:

Kroger bread was five cents a loaf, and you could buy a
Baby Ruth candy bar for the same price.
milk came in a glass quart bottle.
a swingset was not monkey bars, Mickey Mouses and
spaceships, but a long, thick rope swung over a tree
limb and a board to sit on.
we went out the back door to our own gardens, not to
the store, when we needed fresh vegetables.
we knew where our mothers were every day of the week.
almost everyone went to some kind of church on Sunday because J.C. Penney and the meat market knew
that both employees and equipment lasted longer with
a day of rest.
a wooden clothespin made the best teething ring.
air conditioning was simply a cardboard fan with a flat
wooden handle, compliments of Hopewell Funeral
Home and Cemetery.

If you are a younger reader, you may not remember those
"good ol' days," but probably have some recollections of
your own that cause you to sigh in despair at life's complexity. In today's society, most of each day is spent thinking actively. Our brains are on overload most of the time. If
it is true that most of our work is done in our heads, how
can we get away from it? Even more important, how can
we allow simplicity to invade and characterize our lives?

A Little Child Shall Lead Them . . .

One of my favorite pictures shows a barefoot little girl
strolling on the beach, a sand bucket over her right shoulder. Her head is bent in contemplation—and people are following her! The caption, taken from Isaiah 11:6, reads, "And
a little child shall lead them."

In preparation for the writing of this book I have solicited "child stories" from my friend, children's pastor *par excellence* Karen Siddle, and from many young parents of my acquaintance. Pastor Rick Kloos and his wife, Pennie, even offered to lend me their four boys, all under the age of five, until I finished the book! (I declined with gratitude.)

At the church we attend, Pastor Benny Cunningham shepherds the little people's chapel, and his lambs are called K.O.R., "Kids on the Rock." The Rock, of course, is Christ Jesus, the center and theme of Pastor Benny's ministry. So in addition to my other efforts, I have positioned myself as an unseen observer of Pastor Benny's K.O.R. group, snooping for examples of simplicity for this book. I have found them. Some say that experience is the best teacher. I have discovered all over again that children are the best teachers.

Jesus knew this truth well. He considered childlikeness to be an absolute prerequisite for entering the Kingdom of heaven (see Matthew 18:3). This line of thinking was carried on by the apostle Paul in 1 Corinthians 1:

> Where is the wise [man]? Where is the scribe [scholar]? Where is the disputer [philosopher] of this age? Has not God made foolish the wisdom of this world? For . . . the foolishness of God is wiser than men, and the weakness of God is stronger than men. . . . God has chosen the foolish things of the world to put to shame the wise, and God has chosen the weak things of the world to put to shame the things which are mighty.
>
> verses 20–21, 25, 27

God usually uses simple, uncomplicated people. I am amazed that He reached down into the prairies of North Dakota, tagged me and said, "Write." But why am I surprised? That has been His pattern all along. Moses stuttered, but God chose him to lead a nation out of captivity. God called little boy Samuel to be His servant. He taught Gideon, the youngest son in his family and a simple grain farmer, tactics of warfare, and Gideon won a critical and decisive battle. He nudged a little Hebrew girl to bear witness to God's power in Naaman's household. He used David to kill a mighty giant when he was too young for much of anything according to Hebrew culture, could not wrestle and did not know how to fence. He allowed a seven-year-old named Joash to be crowned king so the country of Israel could experience a powerful spiritual revival. He sent Jesus to the world as a helpless baby, for goodness' sakes!

I think young babies and children have their heavenly visas in order before they reach the age of accountability. My belief was reinforced a few years ago when I was called by a nurse to come to the hospital in Madison, South Dakota. A young couple's two-year-old son, Tommie, had an accident and went into arrest on the way to the hospital. After the doctor did a tracheotomy, cutting a hole in his windpipe so he could breathe, medical personnel were able to resuscitate him. Suddenly Tommie looked at his daddy and exclaimed, "Jesus loves me!" with the joy only a two-year-old can exude.

"Who told you that?" his daddy asked.

"He told me. I saw Him," Tommie replied with certainty.

The couple wept as they explained to me that both sets of parents had resisted their marriage, partly because one family was Catholic and one was Jewish. To keep peace, the couple decided never to go to a church or synagogue and never to mention the names *God* or *Jesus*. So they had never said the name of Jesus in front of this child, and had been assured by a Catholic nun, a nurse, that she had not said anything to the child to encourage him to expect to see Jesus during his brief death!

In a newsletter on spiritual growth, Norman Elliott speaks of the simplicity of a child, noting that children are a heritage of the Lord and babies are a gift from God. He tells the story of a three-year-old who insisted that his parents leave the room so he could talk with his newborn sibling.

"Babies come from God," they overheard the little fellow telling the baby. "Hurry up and tell me what God looks like. I'm starting to forget." Children are precious to God, perhaps partly because they have come so recently from Him that their memories are not dulled by time and neglect, or diluted by adult philosophy. It behooves us to nurture such simplicity, the simplicity that is in Christ.

A Biblical Principle

On November 6, 1995, I celebrated the 25th anniversary of my fortieth birthday. I am a survivor. I do not have all the answers, but as I have studied God's Word and observed the little children He holds up as examples of simplicity, I have found a few. As together we explore how God can help us transform our frantic lives into simpler ones, let's look at a biblical principle that can be foundational in our search.

In the beginning, Satan beguiled, tricked, Adam and Eve out of their simple belief in God, and he has been trying to complicate the lives of good people ever since. Paul says,

> I fear, lest somehow, as the serpent deceived Eve by his craftiness, so your minds may be corrupted from the simplicity that is in Christ.
>
> 2 Corinthians 11:3

If life has been complicated for you, that is not from God. God asks for our sincere and pure devotion to Christ—no more, no less. Micah 6:8 puts it like this: "What does the Lord require of you but to do justly, to love mercy, and to walk humbly with your God?"

Contend for the simplicity that is in Christ. In this world you will have to contend, because no one is going to drop

simplicity in your lap. But do not mistake simple-minded-
ness (stupidity, silliness or lack of intellect) for simplicity. There is a vast difference between being a simple
(sincere, uncomplicated, unaffected) believer and being
a simpleton.

"How do I contend?" you ask. In the next few chapters
we will look at many childlike qualities we need to build
into our lives, including childlike love, childlike faith, childlike wonder and a childlike ability to rely completely on
God. But before we do, here are three basic childlike practices we adults need to relearn.

1. *Shut down between your ears.* Make it a point each
day to spend time in a relaxing activity that distracts you;
regularly let yourself become so pleasantly involved in a
leisure activity that you lose track of time.

All children do this naturally, but many of us adults have
lost this critical life skill, and only with practice will we
recover it. For maximum benefit and satisfaction for your
whole person—physical, mental, emotional and spiritual—
and to ensure your sanity, decide to disconnect now and
then. The solution to living well—to living the abundant
life—lies not in new and better technology, but in the selec-
tive *disuse* of it so as to enjoy life in a more emotionally fulfilling way.

My husband, Carl, grew up on Luther Street in the noisy,
congested city of Cleveland, Ohio. The houses were so close
that he could spread his arms out and touch both his house
and the house next door. His retreat to sanity and simplicity was to take long bike rides or to walk to Lake Erie alone.
We need space for individuality.

2. *Find a place for regular refuge and retreat.* I survived
as a pastor's daughter with four brothers, all of us "pew
babies," perhaps partly because my parents did not live in
a parsonage or manse. Instead they found a place in the
country where we Perkins children could run, hit baseballs
without breaking neighbors' windows, ride bikes, grow

things, work in the garden, sell strawberries, have a horse, a dog, some cats, guineas, chickens and even raise turkeys.

Looking back, I remember my childhood "hidey hole," my private refuge. It was an apple tree in the back of the orchard where I could retreat to be quiet, to think, take my doll, pray and talk to God in my own language.

Watch how often the children you know seek out small, sheltered spots in which to sit quietly, observing—or shutting out—the world.

Birds do this. I have watched at the bird feeder outside our bedroom window on the east, in the early morning sun. The young, pale gray dove (symbol of the Holy Spirit and of peace) will not eat amid the clamor and noisy competition of other birds. I saw her this morning, waiting for a quiet moment to eat her breakfast undisturbed.

Figaro, April's cat, always absented herself when company came. For a long time I have wondered where she hid. When I plugged in my printer to start this new book, I found hair and tear, evidence that her hiding place was in the box of 8 1/2" x 11" paper between the computer stand and the printer cabinet. That dark corner offered just enough room to protect her beautiful black-and-white body and to insure her tranquillity.

The Word tells us that God is our refuge and that we can take refuge in the shadow of His wings until disaster has passed (see Psalm 57:1). When we get to our physical places of safety or retreat from distressing and demanding circumstances—and even when we cannot—God can offer peace by His very presence and protection.

3. *Insulate the four walls of your home with quiet time, prayer and peace.* It may not always be possible, but if you can, provide a quiet place for your family to live. If possible, get out of debt. We have become prisoners to payments. God pays all bills He authorizes. Bigger is not always better. Larger houses may mean larger payments producing financial strain. You cannot control the atmosphere "out

there," but you can develop a peaceful climate where you and your family can retreat from the perilous times that are going to get worse.

A successful businessman told me recently, "Our two sons have never wanted for much, but I noticed a void. I suddenly realized that we had never established family devotions. I bought your book *Morning Jam Sessions*, and invited our sons, fifteen and seventeen, and my wife, their mother, to sit down one morning before leaving for school. The clown of the two cajoled, 'What's this, preach? Havin' church?' I read the devotional page for that date, then made a feeble attempt to pray for our family, asking God's help for the day. I realized that my sons had never heard me pray aloud."

Saints and scholars have written whole books about prayer, and its importance in developing simplicity in our lives cannot be overestimated.

Yesterday I talked with my friend Tracy Hamelink on the phone. She told me that the previous evening she had put five-year-old Jennifer on her lap to read her a bedtime story before tucking her in. A picture in the book showed Jesus holding a little girl and saying, "If anyone is mean to you, you must forgive."

Jennifer, a true child of her time, blurted out, "No, Mommy, don't forgive them. Call 911 and they will haul off the mean people!"

A little child shall lead them. . . .

Jennifer led me to look, and I found a "911" that works wonders. Saul, a murderer, was struck blind, but he called 911—Acts 9:11: He prayed! The Lord restored his eyesight, he was filled with the Holy Spirit, his name was changed to Paul and he became a missionary and writer of an impressive portion of the Bible.

In the Old Testament the priest or father of each household applied the blood of a lamb over the lintel and doorposts of his house. I believe that in essence, by faithful prayer, we can do the same. We can draw an invisible blood line around our homes. After Jesus' death on the cross, blood (liquid love) flowed from His side. We have His Word, the assurance that He will protect us. Satan cannot cross the blood line.

"In returning and rest you shall be saved; in quietness and confidence shall be your strength" (Isaiah 30:15). "Rest in the Lord, and wait patiently for Him" (Psalm 37:7). Our homes can be sanctuaries to return to at the end of our hectic days, away "from the snare of the fowler and from the perilous [noisesome, KJV] pestilence" (Psalm 91:3). Our homes can become places to which our families look forward to coming—harbors, shelters, happy places of healing from strife and din.

We Are Becoming

The story is told of two jealous single women who at the invitation of their married friend went to visit. She showed them her wedding pictures, then went on to show off her only child, a homely two-year-old. When the hostess left the room to make tea, she left the child playing unconcernedly in the middle of the floor. Watching her, one visitor remarked cattily to the other, "The child sure is u-g-l-y."

Looking up, the two-year-old declared, "But she sure is s-m-a-r-t!"

It is fortunate that most children, unlike that precocious little girl, are essentially unaware of how much we need to learn from them! At least that makes it easier for us to observe and "correct our courses" in this important area of regaining our simplicity, of becoming like little children in our faith and lifestyles.

Over and over in this book I will remind all of us that we are becoming. "Unless you are converted and become as little children, you will by no means enter the Kingdom of heaven" (Matthew 18:3). Is this why becoming a Christian, getting our passports in order for eternity, is referred to as the "new birth" and "being born again"?

The apostle Paul said it so well:

> Not that I have already attained [all this], or am already perfected; but I press on, that I may lay hold of that for which Christ Jesus has also laid hold of me.
>
> Philippians 3:12

TWO

Capture a Child's Perspective

Think Small

Bigger is better! More! More! Think power! Go for the top! Become the biggest and the best and you will be happy!

These messages bombard us all our lives. Madison Avenue's powerful tentacles reach out through television, radio and print media to convince us that multinational corporate mergers, celebrity status and slickly packaged mega-products from theme parks to election campaigns to Christian outreach methods are the only way to go if we want to be "successful."

But getting back to simplicity involves paring off the unnecessary and discovering the core: What is the meat, the essence of this or that? What is really important? Bigger is not always better. Little things mean a lot. If you don't think so, sit one inch off the center of the piano bench either to the left or right; unless you check your finger placement carefully, the music may be utter chaos! Or shut your eyes and move your finger position just a fraction of an inch on the keyboard of your computer, then open your eyes and try to read what you have typed. What is unavoidably important about either task? The simple fact of having your fingers in the right place!

Even more important: Little is much when God is in it. A child may not be able to quote the verse from Zechariah, but he or she knows the truth of chapter 4:10: "Who has despised the day of small things?" Many a budding entrepreneur got his or her start from a neighborhood lemonade stand or paper route. Many a successful author began by composing grade school poetry or imaginative stories that made the teacher cringe—but held a hint of potential.

How to Think Small

We must try to regain simplicity by seeing things through children's eyes, by capturing their perspective on the world and what happens in it. In this chapter we will look at nine ways to develop a child's perspective by thinking small.

1. Humility Is a Natural Part of a Child's Perspective

The Bible says, "Do not think of yourself more highly than you ought, but rather think of yourself with sober judgment, in accordance with the measure of faith God has given you" (Romans 12:3, NIV). Many folks boast but fail to deliver the goods. Wearing a Harvard T-shirt does not make me a lawyer. Humility is essential in the Kingdom to come.

Matthew 19:30 describes the outcome of humility: "Many who are first will be last, and many who are last will be first" (NIV). Eugene Peterson, author of *The Message* calls this the "Great Reversal." If you have forsaken safety in exchange for taking risks for others and the Kingdom, then when the

Son of God recreates the world and rules gloriously, you who have sacrificed for the Gospel and God's people, large and small, will also rule with Him. The disciples asked Him, "What chance do we have to make it?" Jesus said, "No chance at all if you think you can pull it off yourself. Every chance in the world if you trust God to do it." (Matthew 19:25–26, TM; see also John 15:5.) One translation of Psalm 10 states it this way: "The wicked are so cocksure that they'll never come up for audit. But those recording angels are excellent bookkeepers."

Make no mistake: The meek shall inherit the earth (Matthew 5:5). The plan of salvation is made easy enough for the simple, the fool, the child. "Whosoever shall *call upon the name of the Lord* shall be saved" (Romans 10:13, KJV, italics mine). That one-word prayer, the name *Jesus*, is enough, because *Jesus* means "God saves from every circumstance."

The wicked and mighty King Herod refused to be humble enough to call on the name of Jesus. When he stood in his palace in his royal robes, a large man who denied the Kingship of Jesus, little worms (think small!) ate him right in front of his audience (see Acts 12:20–23). By contrast Daniel, a humble man who was small in his own estimation, prayed three times a day to God the Father, and big lions refused to eat him (see Daniel 6)!

Meekness and humility also imply the quality of being teachable. Young children are teachable, and the wisest man who ever lived, King Solomon, recognized that attribute and tried to imitate it. He talked to God, straight and plain, saying, "I am a little child; I do not know how to go out or come in [carry out my duties]. . . . Give to Your servant [think small!] an understanding heart to judge Your people, that I may discern between good and evil" (1 Kings 3:7, 9).

This teachable attitude was the beginning of Solomon's wisdom, and it can be the beginning of wisdom for us. There is none so blind as he who closes his eyes, and none so deaf as the person who deliberately closes his ears to the truth. The hardest person to deliver a message to is the one who is always talking, never listening. No one has the right to demand to be understood until he has earned the wisdom learned, to know the true Source of all understanding.

2. Think like a Child

Children are transparent. We adults have played the game of bait and switch for so long, we have become mental frauds. We Christian adults, especially, try to make life so complicated. In the Old Testament we read that God gave Moses ten rules. Jesus was even simpler, offering only two rules for life and living: Love God and love people.

Jill Buyea teaches a Sunday school class for nine-, ten- and eleven-year-olds. She surveyed her students to gain their answers to several questions, and sent me the results. Here is a cross-section:

Question: If Jesus walked into the classroom and you could ask Him whatever you wanted, what would you ask?

Answers: "Is it time to go to heaven?"
"What is heaven like?"
"Could You show me heaven?"
"When are You going to take us all to heaven?"
"Can I see my great-grandpa who died in World War II?"
"Could You help me? My mom and dad are divorced and I live with my dad. I love him, but I need my mom, too."

Question: What bothers you most about being a Christian?

Answers: "Reading the Bible."
"Being a pastor's son."

Question: Do you like to pray?

Answers: "Yes, because it's a good feeling."
"Yes, because you get to tell somebody your feelings."
"Yes, 'cause I want everything to go right."

Question: If you could change one thing about the world, what would it be?

Answers: "No school."
"Get all the hatred out of the world."
"No more danger."
"To bring back Carlos and Grandma Joanne."

Try some of these questions on the little people around *you*, for insight into their simple yet profound thought processes.

Several eight-year-olds in an elementary school were asked to write essays about God. One of them, by Danny Dutton, offers a marvelous illustration of a child's uncomplicated thinking. See what you think!

God

One of God's main jobs is making people. He makes them to take the place of the ones who die, so there will always be enough people on earth. He doesn't make grown-ups, just babies. Probably because they are smaller and don't cost so much, and easier to make. He doesn't have time to teach them to talk and walk, so He gives them to mothers and fathers. That works out pretty good.

Another important job that God has is listening to prayers. He is so busy He doesn't even have time to watch TV or listen to the radio, 'cause He's listening to prayers. Don't waste your time asking for anything your parents already said you can't have; He won't do that.

Atheists are people who don't know there is a God. I don't think there are any in my town. None of them go to our church anyway.

Jesus is God's Son. He used to do all the hard work, like walking on water, doing miracles that can't happen, and teaching people who don't want to learn. They got tired of Him preaching to them so they crucified Him. He told His Father to forgive them, because they didn't know what they were doing. God said O.K. and told Him, "You don't have to go out on the road anymore." Now He stays in heaven like a secretary, only more important, of course, and helps His Father out by listening to prayers. He and His Father have it worked out so one of them is on duty all the time.

Don't skip Sunday school. That makes God sad. Anyway, the sun doesn't get warm until after lunch. If you don't believe in God, you will be an atheist, and you will be lonely. Your parents can't go everywhere you go, like summer camp, but God can. He's around when you are scared in the dark, and when big boys throw you into the real deep water, and you can't swim very good.

You shouldn't always think what God can do for you. I figure God put me here and He can take me back anytime He pleases. That's why I believe in God.

Few adults could say it better!

3. Discern like a Child

My husband thinks that small children come standard-equipped with an invisible radar more spiritually sensitive than many adults. Warden Laws of New York State's Sing-Sing Penitentiary occasionally interviewed persons to clean his house, babysit his children or home-school his little daughter. He never hired anyone around whom his children seemed nervous or skittish. Most children's impressions are on target.

Children can spot phonies. They are not bound by titles or labels, nor are they impressed by size, addresses, salaries, degrees or age. They recognize "real."

Jennifer and Bruce Beck's little four-year-old, Lauren, refused to clap for a person who had just sung a solo in children's church. Her mother asked, "Why didn't you applaud like everyone else?"

"I'm not clapping because he's not like Jesus," Lauren explained quickly. "He's bad."

C. M. Ward, a legend among speakers, stayed in our home when preaching in our area. I've heard him say many times, "You can't control what your parents decide to call you when you're born. You are not responsible for your name. But you *are* responsible for what people think of when your name is called."

Children can discern.

4. Don't Value a Package by Its Size or Wrapping

The Son of God made His entrance on this earth, bundled in swaddling clothes, wrapped up in a cobbler's apron, a simple birth to simple earth parents, Joseph and Mary.

Jesus came as a baby, and the heart of God beating in that baby would be broken for you and for me.

Reverend Herbert Lange has said, Jesus "took a child as an example for us to follow (Mark 9:36). He took a small item like a towel, and served (John 13:4). He was meek and humble, never showing off, but showing up when there was a need. He was Almighty, but He didn't act almighty. He was holy, but didn't act 'holier than thou.'"

Grandma Strait and her husband, Lester, were sitting beside the fireplace on Christmas Eve in Port Allegheny, Pennsylvania, when she requested, "How would it be if I opened one of my gifts before Christmas morning? May I open the biggest one?"

Now Lester was always the clown, playing tricks on his wife. So he accommodated her with a mischievous grin. "Sure, honey!"

He handed her a big box inappropriately wrapped in brown paper bags scotch-taped together. She unwrapped the outer box, then a smaller box, then a little pouch. Inside it was a used envelope from a utility bill. Grandma yelled, "Just like you to give me the light bill for Christmas!" and she threw it into the fire.

Quickly Lester grabbed the poker, raked the envelope out and stomped on it with his big field boots. Opening it, he showed Grandma a new, crisp one hundred dollar bill!

5. If You Are Willing to Take a Small Assignment, God May Give You a Bigger One

Over twenty years ago Jack Hayford answered the call to pastor a struggling church in Van Nuys, California, where Sunday morning attendance seldom exceeded one hundred. Today, about ten thousand persons *per week* attend worship services and meetings at the (greatly enlarged) facility.

Someone asked Jack the secret of his church's growth. "I keep looking back to our small beginning," he replied, "the simplicity of how it all started with God's help." Jack Hayford accepted a small assignment, and God gave him a bigger one—and the help he needed to accomplish the task.

I have always wanted to know the names of the "rope holders" who let down that basket containing Paul over the city wall, saving his life (see Acts 9:25). If it had not been for those four, Paul would have been a "basket case" for sure! God give us more rope holders!

We need some "roof climbers," too—people who lend their faith to those who are low on courage. The second chapter of Mark records the story of a crowd so large that a man with palsy (multiple sclerosis, perhaps?) could not get into the house where Jesus was teaching and healing. So four men said, "Borrow our faith." They took tiles off the flat roof and let the man with the palsy and his bed down into the room right in front of Jesus, who both healed and forgave him. I would love to know the names of those four men. God give us more humble, but great, roof climbers!

I am amazed at my own life, that God would see the desire of an eight-year-old girl to write. He reached down to a prairie woman in North Dakota, and prompted her to write about me to Catherine Marshall and *Guideposts* magazine. That Garry Moore would read my story and invite me to be on "To Tell the Truth," and that a publisher would forward publisher Len LeSourd's letter from Jamestown, North Dakota, to Pasadena, Texas, inviting me to write that first little book that is now in fourteen languages, still thrills me.

This is my twelfth book, but before I made the "big-time" (for a Christian author, at least!) I did the janitorial work at a small church in Palm Harbor, without pay. It was a small assignment, but important to God!

6. God Will Work Miracles through You If You Don't Care Who Gets the Credit

This is why Jesus said to pray anonymously (in your closet) and give anonymously. Don't toot your own horn; the parasite will find you and bankrupt you (see Matthew 6). He is doubly blessed who can do something without praise.

The daily devotional *God Calling* has endured for at least two generations now. Two unnamed people listened daily for God's telegrams and prescriptions to help readers find their way, find answers for their personal needs. Have you noticed that some of the best material is written by that same wonderful author, "Unknown"?

Our children's pastor, Benny Cunningham, gave me big news about a small, unknown young man whose story is found in 1 Chronicles 11:22–23. If you would ask the average churchgoer, "Who was Benaiah?" he or she would ask, "Who?"

Most warriors and athletes can function well if they are conditioned or have been working out at the health club before an upcoming event. Benaiah went down into a pit and killed a lion, against all odds, on a snowy day when traction was dangerous and slippery. After that he went on to kill one of his country's enemies, a seven-foot six-inch-tall, lionlike man who had a sword the size of a weaver's beam.

Maybe Benaiah read Psalm 27:1–6 that morning before he went out with the soldiers. Here it is in *The Message*:

> Light, space, zest . . . that's God! So, with Him on my side, I'm fearless, afraid of no one and nothing. When vandal hordes ride down ready to eat me alive, those bullies and toughs fall flat on their faces. When besieged, I'm calm as a baby. When all hell breaks loose, I'm collected and cool. I'm asking God for one thing, only one thing: To live with him in his house my whole life long. I'll contemplate his beauty; I'll study at his feet. That's the only quiet, secure place in a noisy world, the perfect getaway, far from the buzz of traffic. God holds me head and shoulders above all who try to pull me down. Don't quit. Stay with God.

"Stay with God." What a simple way to express a simple, childlike secret. Recognition, praise, glory and pride all fade away in significance when we focus on doing what God tells us—not for any gain of our own, but just because He says so. When we obey, He does do miracles through us!

7. Communicate in Plain Language

When the Rev. David Keaton became the pastor of one of our neighboring churches in Dunedin, Florida, an old patriarch advised him, "Don't rely on gimmicks, just plow corn." The world is aware of the fact that Billy Graham survived to share the Gospel over the years because he preached the same, simple message of salvation with no fluff.

Before Catherine Marshall died she coached me, "Betty, the poor man will never go to the rich man's market, but the rich man will come to the poor man's market. If when you write, you write in simple, plain words and terms that children can understand, you will have a full market. If you use large, impressive, hard-to-understand words, you will impress only the educated, limit the people you can help and limit your book sales. Think small."

Benjamin Franklin called it "ink power": "Give me 26 simple lead soldiers and I will conquer the world [with the] power of the simple alphabet and penciled words."

One of my favorite small books is *The Wisdom of the Sandbox* by Cynthia Lewis. Cynthia gets her material from her three muses, Anya, Alexandra and Aaron. The tiny, four-by-five-inch book is crammed full of really important things her three children—her guiding geniuses—have taught her.

8. Place People above Possessions, Status, Money or Fame

An evangelist once preached in a very small church, and ended the service by asking: "Will anyone here answer the call to go overseas to the poor who need Christ?" As he did so, he looked around the sanctuary, wondering if God knew what He was doing in directing His servant to give such an appeal to an "insignificant" congregation of small children and old ladies.

Suddenly the old pump organ up in the balcony stopped its music, and the evangelist exclaimed to himself, "Oh no! That organist must be eighty years old! Surely she's not going to answer the call!"

What the man of God failed to see was that a small thirteen-year-old boy had been lying on his stomach on the floor, pumping air to the organ. Now he came down the aisle to obey the call to missions. The boy became the great missionary David Livingstone.

When Jesus was on earth, He did not hobnob with snobs; He gravitated toward need. One day He and His disciples traveled by boat across the lake to the region of the Gergesenes. As they landed the boat on a bank, two men ran out of the cemetery looking wild and frightening. Jesus cast demons out of them both, commanding the devils to enter into a herd of swine. The pigs, newly infested, promptly ran headlong into the sea and drowned.

Meanwhile, Jesus did not tell the two men to go on television, develop doctrines or write books bragging about what He had done for them. Instead He sent them back to their families (see Matthew 8). Can you imagine the joy in those homes when their husbands and fathers arrived sane, peaceful and in their right minds?

But the farmers who owned the pigs were not glad for the deliverance and healing of their neighbors. Instead they wanted to mob the Lord for the loss of their food and income! They loved pork more than people!

We need to invest in people, needy people. We must wear our possessions and our aspirations to status, money and fame like loose garments with no buttons, willing to take them off and give them away.

9. Invest in Children

"Let the little children come to me, and do not hinder them," said Jesus, "for the kingdom of heaven belongs to such as these" (Matthew 19:14, NIV).

A pastor in Hot Springs, Arkansas, the third-largest retirement community in the United States, realized that his church was unbalanced. The average age in the community was 65, and his church's population reflected that. He decided that the congregation needed to rediscover babies.

One Sunday he brought several babies into the sanctuary during worship and said, "Let them down, let them alone, let them do what they want unless they start to endanger themselves or damage a musical instrument. Before you point a finger at them, reach out your hand, to Jesus and to them." Then he continued with the service.

Some in the congregation thought this was great; most nearly had nervous breakdowns. But what an eye-opener! The older people began to see the needs of little ones and eventually adjusted their ministry and the outreaches of their church accordingly. Now many young couples attend that church.

How can you invest in children? First, never forget what it was like to be a child. Many adults act as though they were born grown up, with no memory or understanding of the tenderness of small hearts. The apostle Paul was willing to admit that when he was a child, he "spoke as a child . . . understood as a child . . . thought as a child" (1 Corinthians 13:11). We need to do the same.

The second investment in children follows hard on the heels of the first: *Because* you remember what it was like to be a child, be patient with children. Every age and stage is necessary for their development, just as it has been necessary for ours. A three-and-a-half-year-old may be so insecure as to make some necessary, practical activities difficult for himself and his parents. Yet a four-year-old may seem brashly secure and much too confident, out of bounds emotionally and motorwise. You and I went through the same stages. And watching the natural growth process is a good parable about the way we develop spiritually!

One additional thought about the growth process: Never deny children a childhood. I know a small girl who waits by our house for the school bus each morning. She is the oldest little girl I have ever met. Skipping stages, or requiring children to grow up too fast, can cause them to be like plants: Too much fertilizer burns them up; too much water causes mold.

This book is all about the process of becoming a person of simplicity. A small child is becoming, becoming *some-*

one and *something.* Help him or her retain simplicity by not passing on our twin adult "viruses"—rushing and complexity.

The third way you can invest in children is to be good to them. Remember, Jesus *loved* the little children.

Why wouldn't a person be good to children? Because children (like adults) can be trying. At church a while ago I overheard the frustrated mom of a misbehaving four-year-old joke, "I've been thinking of doing what Hannah did with her son. She took him to the temple and *left him there!*"

But it is incredible what a mother will put up with for the sake of her child. I read the following quotation by Washington Irving in the monthly newsletter *In Other Words* of Dr. Raymond McHenry:

> There is an enduring tenderness in the love of a mother to a son, that transcends all other affections of the heart. It is neither to be chilled by selfishness, nor daunted by danger, nor weakened by worthlessness, nor stifled by ingratitude. She will sacrifice every comfort to his convenience; she will surrender every pleasure to his enjoyment. She will glory in his fame and exalt in his prosperity; and if adversity overtake him, he will be the dearer to her by misfortune; and if disgrace settle upon his name, she will still love and cherish him; and if the world beside cast him off, she will be all the world to him.

Do we treat our spiritual children, our little sons and daughters, brothers and sisters in the local and world-wide family of God, like that?

Be careful how you treat children. I sincerely believe that the recording angels keep record of our attitudes toward youngsters when no one is observing. And God neither slumbers nor sleeps; an unseen, all-seeing eye is watching you.

Jesus said that if anyone mistreats one of His little ones, it would be better that a millstone be cast around his neck and he be cast into the deepest sea (see Matthew 18:6).

Small Beginnings . . . Big Source

When I look at the source of light above my computer, I ask myself, Is it the filament in the bulb that produces bright light? No, it is not even the cord that plugs into the wall, or the power line coming into the house. The transformer is not the source of light, nor is the turbine that produces the electricity as the water courses over the dam, nor are the rapids before the dam. The bright light finds its source in the still waters at the head of the stream—a small, calm beginning.

Some farmers in a small community rescued two boys from a burning house. One of them was Charles Wesley, and the other was John. Small beginnings. . . .

"Go to the ant, you sluggard," advised Solomon. "Consider her ways and be wise" (Proverbs 6:6).

Ben Kinchlow, who now has his own telecast, started out driving a car for Pat Robertson. Small beginnings. . . .

A small, thin boy named Bob Hoskins sang with his sister at a children's camp in Indiana. He grew up to serve God as one of the directors of the International Correspondence Institute and to wield great influence for the Christian faith in the Middle East, including war-torn, hard-to-reach Beirut. Small beginnings. . . .

I got a telephone call from a small boy named Marty Batt, inviting me to come and tell my story to his school, Our Lord's Academy in Tarpon Springs, Florida. Knowing that this child had no authority to extend such an invitation, I thanked him but did not take him seriously. But several days later I wondered: Was his call God's nudge toward a miracle? As I drove along the highway that day, the sky blackened. Suddenly the clouds parted and a tiny rainbow became beautifully clear. When I returned home I called Marty's principal and arranged to speak to students and parents the following week. I am still getting responses from parents who came that night and thanked me for relieving their fear of death.

Marty was not afraid to speak up, and he did not even know there was a procedure to secure speakers for school assemblies. Small beginnings. . . .

Let Jesus be your Source. "'Not by might nor by power, but by My Spirit,' says the Lord Almighty" (Zechariah 4:6). Rest in Him, the Source; rewind and reconsider. Sometimes God saves the best till last, when we have tried it all and failed, realizing we are but children.

Think small.

THREE

Believe like a Child

Faith

Adult human beings live with the standard equipment of five senses: sight, smell, hearing, touch and taste. But I believe children come with eight. The extra three are faith, wonder and creative imagination. We will look at faith in this chapter, and save the other two for discussion in chapter 4.

Yes, I believe children emerge from the womb with faith. God gives them the first breath, but they have to have faith to keep breathing for the next eighty years. Babies are born with faith to put their lips to a breast they have never seen or felt and expect life-giving nourishment! Babies sense that if they cry, someone will eventually come and change their diapers or cuddle away their fears. Babies have inborn faith.

Karen Siddle told me she was amazed when June Marie, one of her seven-year-old students, told her, "Miss Karen, there are three kinds of believers: unbelievers, make-believers and true believers." Out of the mouths of babes. . . . God gave Jesus a name above every name, and children around the world sing it: "Jesus loves me, this I know, for the Bible tells me so." Children believe God and they believe the Bible, no doubt about it.

What Is So Special about Childlike Faith?

When Christians discuss Jesus' command that believers become like little children (see Matthew 18:3), I think we *assume* He meant for us to be like children in the faith department. As we have already seen, however, for Jesus to point to childlikeness as a goal for all Christians implies that we are to become like them in many areas, and not just faith.

But the virtues of childlike faith were certainly high on Jesus' list of priorities for us to grasp, so let's examine them.

1. *Children are not cynical; they trust easily.* Children believe everything they hear and anyone who says it. My friend Pennie Kloos told me, "I have to be very careful what I tell my four little men, all under the age of five. I could tell them that a big monster lives in a small box and they would believe me. I could offer to trade my big nickel for one of my boys' tiny dimes, and he would think he was getting a good deal, because he trusts me."

The simplest yet highest form of faith is trust—in the message and the messenger.

I had two adorable grandfathers who were exact opposites. Dad Perky was a tall, straight Englishman, a school-teacher who dealt in absolutes, data, facts, and said very little.

Dad Burns, a freelance carpenter, was a little smaller in stature. He was spontaneous, with a wee bit of Scotch and Irish blended with a pinch of imp. If things got out of hand at his house when we were there (and we were there a lot), or if people became quarrelsome or started debating politics or religion, he would jump to his feet and start a little routine: He would hop on one foot, then skip around, pretending to play a fiddle at a square dance. This was his signal: "Enough," and we honored and obeyed his wishes.

Dad Burns could tell us anything and we believed him. He once told my little brothers, "Eat your spinach. It will grow hair on your chests." We believed him so completely that I would *not* eat my spinach. I had illusions that someday I would go to England, where our family had roots, and be a princess in a castle. I did not want hair on my chest! Only when we were older did it dawn on our more cynical, sophisticated minds that Dad Burns had absolutely no hair on his chest, and he ate his spinach!

A short time ago I was returning by air from Rapid City, South Dakota, to Tampa when the plane began to vibrate and drop during severe turbulence. The pilot announced that the course of our flight plan would have to be altered since severe thunderstorms and a tornado had been spotted over Nashville.

Looking across the aisle I noticed a young mother busying herself with paperwork, writing and making notes. On the aisle near me sat her young daughter, probably four years old, with very large and fearful eyes. Just then the plane lurched and she reached toward me and asked, "What's wrong?"

Under my breath I whispered, "Dear Jesus, don't let me give her the wrong answer." So the Holy Spirit gave me a reply that was smarter than me.

"The wind is playing with those big, white clouds," I told her. "They are just getting a little noisy, that's all."

"O.K.," she sighed, and in less than three minutes she had rested her head on her little arm and fallen soundly asleep on the armrest of her seat. Talk about trusting!

Before we landed in Tampa, I wrote a note and asked her mother for permission to use the illustration in this chapter. In reply the mother, Mrs. Steven (Vanessa) Lund of Huntley, Montana, wrote: "[The importance of childlike trust] is a message we all need to remember. Her name is

Shiloh. She was named for her Saviour. The word refers to the Messiah and means 'bringer of peace and prosperity.' May God grant you peace and prosperity in your work."

Oh, that we adults could curb our cynicism and "know-it-all" fears! Oh, that we could be calmed into accepting the peace and prosperity God intends for us by exercising trusting, childlike faith!

2. *Children take God and His Word at face value.* God said it, I believe it. That's faith!

Eight-year-old Jeff loved playing softball. His dad promised to give him twenty dollars for every home run.

At a Saturday game shortly after his dad made that promise, Jeff was rounding third base.

"Stop! Don't go home," the third base coach shouted. Jeff totally ignored his coach and slid in home.

"Why did you disobey my call?" the coach questioned Jeff in some anger.

"My dad told me he'd give me twenty dollars for every home run," Jeff replied without hesitation. "I believe in my dad!"

Oh, that we could follow as closely the instructions of our heavenly Father!

Children believe so easily. If God said it, that is good enough for them. They don't know it "cannot be done," so I am sure God even bends the rules to accommodate their sanctified imaginations.

Bernard (Bernie) Mitchell was pastoring the church little three-year-old Kristi and her parents attended. One day Kristi became very ill.

"Hurry, take me to church and let Jesus touch me, and I'll get well," she insisted. When her parents questioned her, they learned that when they had told her to respect the church because it was God's house, she had also believed that Bernie was Jesus because he lived at the church.

After clearing up the misunderstanding, Kristi's parents showed admirable respect for their daughter's childlike faith in taking her to the church. Pastor Mitchell did lay hands on her and pray for her, and she was instantly well.

One night my telephone rang at 10:30. When I answered, a little voice said, "My dog Buffey is having seizures. The medicine the vet gave her is not working. Will you pray for Buffey?"

I go to bed at 9:00 P.M., so I was too startled and sleepy to pray an intelligent prayer for a sick puppy, but I tried. God honored the child's faith; I got a letter five days later telling me the dog was well!

Unless we become as little children in our faith, we will not qualify for the Kingdom! "You [God] have hidden these [many] things from the wise and prudent and revealed them to babes." Those words are not suggestions from some philosopher or theologian, but direct quotes from the Son of God (see Luke 10:21 and Matthew 11:25). Can we be childlike enough to take them at face value?

When Karen Siddle was a children's pastor in Orlando, she was having prayer time with a group of little ones. Little Aaron came up and told her, "I'm sick. Pray for me."

Karen anointed him with oil according to James 5:14–16: "Pray over [the one who is sick], anointing him with oil in the name of the Lord. And the prayer of faith will save the sick, and the Lord will raise him up."

The following morning Aaron's mother called. "Karen, you've got to come to our home. Aaron is very sick, with a fever higher than 103 degrees. The doctor told us to bring him to the hospital, but he refuses to go. He says you prayed for him and Jesus will heal him. Come and go with us to take him to the hospital. He'll go for you."

When Karen arrived she asked Aaron, "How you doin', bud?"

"I'm going to be O.K., Miss Karen."

Considering his "face-value" faith, Karen said she did not have the nerve to tell him he had to go to the hospital, but she was afraid not to.

"Let's wait till noon," she suggested to his mother. By noon the fever was gone.

I am not suggesting that we should routinely disobey parents or good doctors, but this child believed, and what he believed happened. I think it is significant for us to study the fact that the very young take things simply by faith, at face value, without questioning. How we need to grasp the magnitude of the simplicity of God's Word. It may look like mere black words on white paper, but it contains all we need to survive and thrive on earth. And it contains the words of eternal life as well.

3. *Because children believe (have faith) in angels, I think angels minister to them frequently.* Norman and Naomi Branvold live in Miracle Valley, Arizona, with their two young daughters, Faye and Jane. When Faye was fifteen and Jane was only five, their small town was terrorized by a burglar whom the police department had been unable to apprehend. Fear grew as talk about the burglar spread around the community.

Norman had to travel to Texas, and his wife and girls were nervous without him. Even though they had intended to take an extended trip to North Dakota while he was away, they decided one evening shortly after he left to cancel their plans, concerned about leaving their house unattended.

That night Naomi had locked the doors and the two girls were sitting by a table. Little Jane saw an angel come through the door, though it did not open. She described him as having brown hair and holding a sword. She followed him as he walked through every room in the house.

"I will come back when you go away and protect your home," he told her.

How did he know they were planning a trip? Why did the older daughter not see him or hear him?

Naomi and the girls went ahead with their trip, and no harm came to their place while they were away.

My brother Marvin works with a young woman who teaches four- and five-year-olds in a Presbyterian church. One day little C. J. (all boy) asked the class to pray for his granny.

"She has cancer and all her hair fell out," he told them.

C. J.'s mother later told the teacher that several days after C. J.'s prayer request, a nurse called from the intensive care unit to tell the family to come to the hospital because Granny was dying. C. J.'s mother called him inside from playing and told him, "We must go to the hospital. Granny is dying. She will go to heaven in a few minutes."

"Not!" said C. J., and ran back out the door.

His mother went after him to explain the seriousness of the matter, but C. J. would not hear it.

"Granny is not going to die," he told her simply.

"How do you know?" his mother asked.

"When I was playing in the yard, I asked Jesus to make her all better," C. J. replied. "Jesus told me, 'Granny's gonna be fine.' I saw Him and His angel. They were up above the tree and they both wore white dresses that were on fire. I told Him that I wanted to fly, and He let me fly way up in the sky above the house, then put me down in the porch swing."

While C. J.'s mother was trying to discount his wild story, the phone rang. It was the nurse again. "Your mother is up and wants to go home."

I do not know if I believe C. J.'s story, but how *do* you explain Granny's immediate recovery?

The Word of God tells us that all children have guardian angels watching over them (see Mathew 18:10). Hebrews 1:14 tells us that angels are "ministering spirits, sent forth to minister for them who shall be heirs of salvation" (KJV). Little children are heirs of salvation, but so are believing adults. Could it be that we miss out on the ministry of angels because we are too "mature" to expect their help?

4. *Children expect Jesus to return momentarily.* I received a letter over a year ago from a woman named Marge

Green who explained that she and her husband had moved to the Palm Harbor area and wanted to get acquainted with me. On finding out that we had mutual friends in Bernie and Lois Mitchell, I asked the Mitchells to go with me to meet the Greens in their parsonage home near the New Life Missionary Church.

What a find to discover that the Greens have six small sons! Instead of making the usual getting-acquainted remarks, I could not resist telling Marge that I was doing this book on things we learn about simplicity from children.

"You're in the right place," she laughed. "I'm amazed how much our little guys retain from listening to sermons. While I cooked lunch today, our six-year-old, Jonathan Edward, was poking the touch-tone buttons of our phone. I explained that we don't play with the phone."

"I'm not playing with the phone, Mother," he said. "I'm calling the Antichrist."

"What's his phone number?" Marge asked, going along with his game.

"Dad gave it to us in his sermon," replied Jonathan. "It's 666."

"What will you tell him when you get him, Jonathan?" Marge quizzed him.

"I plan to tell him, 'You're not Jesus, but He's coming!'"

If that was not a declaration of expectation, I don't know what is!

My cousin Peggy Perkins has just suffered a painful divorce, and her two-year-old, Amber, notices that daddies pick up other children at the nursery school. One afternoon, upon returning to their apartment, Amber started to cry, sighing, "Mommy, I want a daddy." Peggy explained to her that their daddy was gone, but that Jesus was their wonderful Daddy.

"Then where is He?" Amber asked.

"He's in heaven."

Little Amber raised the kitchen window and yelled loudly, "Daddy, come home!"

Oh, to have a child's sense of reverent immediacy! As times become more perilous, I have found myself making the same earnest cry. "Even so, come, Lord Jesus" (Revelation 22:20). The Word tells us that unto those who look for Him He shall appear the second time. We must expect His coming again, just as Mary, Joseph, Anna, Simeon and other believing Jews expected the Messiah when He was born in the manger in Bethlehem that first time. We need to look for His coming again with the same eagerness that little ones look for and expect Christmas.

A Measure of Faith for Each of Us

Someone remarked to me that I have had many prayers answered lately. It is true. I am grateful for the way God has come to our rescue in several ways. I believe it is because while writing this book on simplicity, I have become His child again. Yes, theologically I have been His child since my conversion, but now I am becoming more childlike.

I heard myself praying recently, "I appreciate You, Jesus." It was not profound, but it was heartfelt, simply the only way I could express my true feeling. As I said earlier, I thrive on appreciation. If one of my children appreciates something I do for him or her, you can be sure I will keep on doing what I can to help, please and ensure his or her happiness. Our Father God is no different.

On Palm Sunday at our church in Clearwater, approximately six hundred of us wrote our deepest personal needs on small pieces of red paper and nailed them to a large cross. The person in charge read Colossians 2:14, which tells how Jesus took away the things that were "contrary to us," and nailed them to His cross.

I was amazed at the spectacular, almost unbelievable answers to prayer that followed. And almost every one of them happened to children, babes, not young in age but young in their faith, saved only a short time. They were not hindered by years of experience and did not know the "mechanics" of theology and ministry over which some Christians stumble into cold-hearted sophistication. They just believed for answers to their needs and prayers.

One such man, Vincent, was healed of shingles. At two in the morning after Palm Sunday, he awakened with a sensation of burning inside. God was letting him know that Jesus had healed him while he slept. The shingles are gone.

Mr. Seidler, who had not been a Christian for long, had suffered chest pains with a heart condition. Shortly after that Palm Sunday, he realized that for the first time in months he was free from pain. He is now enjoying a normal life.

His wife, Barbara, had a ruptured back disc. She nailed that contrary condition to the cross. The next morning, without thinking, she bent over and tied her own shoes. Later the same day, thinking her earlier feat was too good to be true and that she should prove her new abilities, she raked her whole yard, all without pain.

You may be reading this and complaining, "I don't have faith for my need. I wish I could have the faith of a child that Jesus spoke of."

You do. We all do. If you have ever licked a sticky piece of paper one inch square and attached it to the upper right corner of an envelope, you have faith. Isn't it ridiculous to think that for only 32 cents you can hire a red, white and blue truck complete with driver to take that letter to the airport where a four-million-dollar plane complete with pilot and crew will take it to Uncle Joe in New Jersey in only four days? That is ridiculous faith. But you have it—you have silly, childlike faith in that small stamp.

Take an even more basic example. Last night you reached over in the dark to push up a four-cent piece of plastic, thereby working magic and changing darkness into light. That was naked, basic faith—faith in that light switch. What makes you think that light switch will really work? A small measure of faith.

The Bible says we all have faith. "God has dealt to each [man and woman] a measure of faith," Paul told us in Romans 12:3. Faith comes by hearing, and hearing by the Word of God, spoken or written (see Romans 10:17).

But faith is a coin with two sides. Side one is that faith comes "not of works [our actions] lest anyone should boast" (see Ephesians 2:9). Yet side two is, "Faith without works is dead" (see James 2:17). Yes, faith is a gift from God, dealt out by Him. But to be worth anything, our faith must be activated by our wills. We must choose to act on it. A line from one of our choir anthems says it all: "Faith is stepping out on nothing and landing on something."

Childlike faith: It is a gift. But if we fail to use it, we not only grieve our loving Father; we cheat ourselves of the blessings He so longs to give us.

FOUR

Respond like a Child, Part 1

Wonder and Creative Imagination

n the past sixteen years of travel I have spoken to all age levels of people in 49 out of the 50 states. Each audience, and each person in each audience, responds differently. Some of the material I use may cause certain people to sit on the edge of their seats, while other faces (particularly adult ones) look dull, spoiled and bored, as if I have told them white chalk has just been discovered!

From his many speaking experiences, my husband observes that sharing a new concept with jaded, "So what?" type adults is about as fruitful and rewarding as lighting a firecracker with a wet fuse!

Children, by contrast, possess eager vision, creative imaginations, a yen for the magic in life, a hunger to understand both the visible and the invisible. They are always asking who, where, when, what and why?

As I said in chapter 3, I believe little children have eight senses, not the usual five. We have already discussed the first extra sense, faith. In this chapter we will look at wonder and creative imagination, two hallmark child responses, and in chapter 5 we will examine another response, enthusiasm. We need to examine these qualities and think about how we adults can recapture them so we do not lose our zest for living. We need to see how we can redevelop wonder, creative imagination and enthusiasm in our adult mindsets as part of our quest to build simplicity into our lives.

Here is what I have gleaned about wonder and creative imagination as I have studied children over the past two years. I present it "cafeteria-style"!

Wonder

I am like a child on July 4th. I cannot get enough of sparklers, cherry bombs and firecrackers. I am patriotic, I love America and I love the boom of a firecracker. Last year in a package of 24 I found one fizzle, but I did not quit lighting firecrackers. I enjoyed celebrating with the rest of the package.

Wonder is something like that. The *American Heritage Dictionary* uses words like *awe, astonishment, surprise, admiration* and *curiosity* to describe it. And I would add that wonder is not easily quenched.

A pastor friend told Carl and me about a recent Christmas play held at the church he serves. A doll had represented the baby Jesus in the manger scene during all the rehearsals, but the directors, without telling the children involved, substituted a real, live baby for the final production. About ten minutes into the play the baby stretched and yawned. One little boy exclaimed in loud wonder, "Mom, Jesus is alive!" It was like an Easter pageant at Christmas.

Not all wonder has such a spiritual outcome, of course. Two of my little brothers took umbrellas and, pretending they were paratroopers, jumped from the roof of the cow shed. One was pretty successful, but the other landed in a "cow dab."

When our dad questioned their silly, boyish reasoning, one of my brothers said he approached the jump wondering, *What if we jump and nothing happens?* The other had decided to jump based on the question "What if we don't jump, and something might have happened?"

The first philosophy indicated a hesitant gamble, but the second bespoke wonder. Too many adults have lost the life-giving, invention-inspiring wonder and curiosity that are so typical of small children, and our world is poorer because of it.

Dr. James Barnhill told me he is investing in and enjoying his seven-year-old daughter's sense of wonder.

"Watching her grow up is teaching me to enjoy each day, one day at a time," he says. "[The days] pass so fast."

Have you taken time to look—really look—at a starry sky lately? To ask "Why?" when you see a strange and marvelous sight? Have you been brave enough to express your astonishment and surprise at something new, even though you might "lose face"?

These are bottom-line challenges. To answer them positively means that maybe, just maybe, you are starting to get a handle on what simplicity could look like in your life.

Creative Imagination

Before babysitters, Nintendo, video machines and television, all children had creative imaginations. Some still do. But how sad to hear a story like that of our friend who took her ten-year-old nephew to Disney World and had him ask, after nine expensive, exhausting hours, "Is that all?"

Years ago you could put a child in an empty room and he or she would find something to draw on, climb up or pretend with. Unfortunately, too many of today's children and adults have been overexposed to the spectacular and the supernatural, and spoiled by the convenient. We could learn a lot from the creative ability of young, unspoiled, simple children.

Over the past couple of years I have spotted three ways in which creative imagination manifests in children. Here they are.

1. Children Dream with Creative Imagination

"Your place is where your dreams are," says a character in the movie *Iron Will*.

In the church in New Castle, Indiana, where I played the piano for several years, two little girls named Cathy and Carol Ann loved to pretend to play the piano as I did, their fingers flying across the back of the pew in front of them. Cathy and Carol Ann both grew up with musical abilities. They found their places.

Let kids dream and imagine. Pretending is a form of faith, and a sanctified imagination can point a child toward greatness and incredible accomplishments. Being children works; that is the way we start. And using our creative imaginations plays a vital role in helping us to be all God intends us to be.

The son of a famous couple we all know was the oldest little boy I have ever met. He had to be serious, dressed up and a good performer because of his parents' profession. At forty he decided to "be his child," so he left his wife and two children to act out the childhood he felt he had missed. His wife held steady for two years until he grew from childhood to maturity. I saw God in her.

The moral? Let children be children and dream children's dreams while they are small and young. Dreaming and pretending are part of the work God has given them to do; dreaming and pretending feed their ambitions and hopes for the future. Never stunt their emotional and spiritual growth by forcing them to act grownup too soon. And don't spoil their dreams by constant analysis and vicarious hopes of your own. Life gets serious soon enough—it takes time to be a child.

2. Children See with Creative Imagination

When I flew into the airport at Green Bay, Wisconsin, our friends Paul and Tracy Hamelink and their five-year-old daughter, Jennifer, were on hand to meet me. As I came out of the jetway, Jennifer ran enthusiastically toward me calling, "Aunt Betty!" I hugged her and asked, "Do you like watching airplanes at the airport?"

"No," she replied decisively, "I like to ride 'em." Whether or not that had ever been a reality was irrelevant to Jennifer.

Later on Sunday afternoon Paul told me, "I get so much sermon material from listening to Jennifer and learning from her. Children see differently, creatively. When we moved from Missoula, Montana, she insisted on bringing an old, pink, worn-out, dirty bear. It was a source of embarrassment when we moved in. But wouldn't it be great if only we could look at people and failures the way Jennifer looked at that unsightly pink bear?"

Ask any child, "What was the most exciting assembly you remember in school?" Most of them will tell you, "The magician." It is no wonder books of fairy tales, nursery rhymes and Mother Goose stories have survived and thrived for generations: They are full of magical, incredible happenings that stimulate a child's creative way of seeing.

I was always something of a kid at heart, long before I began realizing the need to return simplicity to my life. So even my adult creative imagination turns on when I read fairy tales. The people who write them have to be divinely inspired. Those stories have double meanings, although each reader takes away his or her own unique interpretations.

Consider with me the story of the "Three Little Pigs." The big bad wolf (the devil) came to the door and bluffed, "Let me in, or I'll huff and I'll puff and I'll blow your house in." Satan is still using deception and bluffs on God's children. And think about the pigs' three houses. The stick house and the straw house collapsed, but the house built of brick (the one "built upon the rock") stood fast.

Creative imagination. What about the story of the "Gingerbread Man"? He ran away from the little old woman and the little old man, "and I can run away from you, I can, I can," he told the fox. In the end the fox (Satan?) tricked him into climbing onto his tail, then onto his back to cross the river. The fox, pretending to assist the little cookie, then insisted that the gingerbread man ride on his head so he would not get wet. When they were midstream, the fox tipped back his head and ate the cocky, gullible gingerbread man.

Do you have young people in your house who have run away from their "little old woman and little old man"? Perhaps you have spent twenty years loving them and thousands of dollars to educate them. Don't give up; just pray, pray, pray.

It would take more than one page to glean the lessons from the story of "Little Red Riding Hood" who was hoodwinked by the big, bad wolf (Satan strikes again!). Her downfall was when he dressed up and fooled her into coming into his bedroom. Get out your fairy tale book and read it. Scripture warns us that "the devil walks about like a roaring lion, seeking whom he may devour" (1 Peter 5:8). Use your creative, childlike imagination, and find lessons for your own life and the people around you.

But don't think, "Kids never see those things in fairy tales. They're just stories." One boy told me that the moral of "Mary Had a Little Lamb" was, "Keep your nose clean and your record white." And my youngest brother, Gary, asked an insightful, creative question one time as I held him on my lap and read the story of "Humpty Dumpty": "Why didn't they ask the *King* to put Humpty Dumpty together again, instead of asking his horses and his men?" Why indeed? But how true of human nature to go everywhere else but to the Source, our King, who alone "[has] the words of eternal life" (John 6:68).

Perhaps speaker Andy Stanley's interpretation of the story of Pinnochio offers the best fairy-tale illustration of an adult who uses his creative imagination. "The more Pinnochio lied," Andy reminded those of us in his audience, "the longer his nose grew. What if every time you walked into a place you should not be, your feet grew? Would you wear a size 74 shoe? And what if when you watched things you shouldn't see, your eyeballs enlarged so that when you walked into church on Sunday, you had to hold them in your hands because they had bulged out so far from their sockets?"

Now that is a creative picture for you!

Have we as mature adults lost our luster for the simple things that are lasting and meaningful? Have we been so overstimulated by television evangelists, "hype" tapes and seminars that we have substituted them for digging out the Word, acknowledging the authority of the Bible? There is no substitute for developing our spiritual creativity in private times of worship. It is not really a bad thing to be quiet, without noise, without background music, without turning on the "boob tube" as soon as we walk in the front door.

Wanda Austin is a beautiful young woman who sings in our choir. She lost her sight a few years ago.

"It has simplified my life," she says. "I am not distracted by looking at people's responses or their clothing, but am keen to the love you can feel in the simple tone of their voices." Wanda is not distracted during choir practice, but zeroes in on memorizing the words.

I asked her how she coped with this sudden change in her life.

"It was a simple solution," she told me. "I had to depend for a while on my family, like a child. Then—" She pulled an ivory-colored strip of paper from her purse. "Feel this. Can you feel the bumps?"

I rubbed the paper. Wanda explained that it was Philippians 4:13 in Braille. "When I get frightened or disoriented, I rub this almost like Aladdin's lamp," she confided. "'I can do all things through Christ who strengthens me.'"

Wanda has learned a new, creatively imaginative way of "seeing." Like other children of God who have recovered the simplicity of the childlike response, she can "walk by faith, not by sight" (2 Corinthians 5:7).

Perhaps you, like many little children, were frightened by stories of giants. Maybe you are feeling frightened by giants today—the giants of finance, fear or sin. Jesus can help you use your God-given creative imagination to "see" those giants for what they really are—powerless and puny in comparison to His might.

Decide today that your personal giants will not intimidate you. Our pastor, Steve Lambert, offered this good counsel: "Give up your right to own your own problems. Your problems are God's now that you are His child. The battle is the Lord's. The giant of fear will loom large at you, but don't back down."

The simplicity of a child's creative imagination, redeveloped in your life by the power of the Holy Spirit, can change the way you deal with all the problems and people in your life.

3. Children Give with Creative Imagination

If only we could give as children do. I spoke at a little Methodist church in Apalachicola, Florida. The pastor had two small sons. The youngest helped me set up my book table, and during the course of the weekend I felt like a kid again, playing and talking with those two little chaps.

As I left, the pastor's young wife handed me a sack containing something that the younger boy had made for me. On the way home I stopped for gasoline, and decided to open the sack. I could not hold back a grin. Inside was a misshapen plastic container like one of the men's urinal bottles used by hospital patients. On the front were scrawled the letters A P A L A C H I C O L A. In the bottle was a printed note that read, "This is for pencils and scissors."

I love that little item, given out of the creativity of a young, spontaneous heart.

When Carl and I moved from a four-story Victorian house into the little four-room place where we now live, we got rid of a lot of large items. But the things we kept were the meaningful things, like that pencil holder—things that represented simple love shown by the giver.

Be as creative as a child in your giving. After a telecast, an elderly woman came behind the set to meet me.

"I would like to read some of your books, but I didn't bring any money with me," she said.

"I didn't bring any books with me," I told her, "but when I get home I'll mail one to you."

And I did. I put together a sequence of three books. Inside I wrote a note, "Happy Mother's Day. No charge." I placed the books into a padded mailer and sent them off with childish joy in my heart for sending her what I hoped would be a delightful surprise.

Several days later I received my package back. It was marked, "Return to Sender. I didn't order these, don't have funds to pay for them."

She had not even opened the package! The books were autographed, so I could not give them to anyone else. I had spent money on the postage, and on the books, and had really inconvenienced myself to prepare that surprise for her. I was hurt.

But it made me realize all over again how Jesus was inconvenienced for us. He prepared wonderful gifts—the gifts of salvation and reconciliation—and millions of people never bother to open them.

Still, He does not take the gifts back. And He does not stop giving to us, because giving is part of His nature.

He wants creative, imaginative giving to be part of our natures, too. Make giving to others part of your life.

Having the Mind of Christ

In your lifetime you will spend four months tying your shoes, eight months opening junk mail, one year looking for misplaced objects and two years returning phone calls unsuccessfully. Budget your time, but make time to be full of wonder toward God (that's worship!) and creatively imaginative as you look at the world and people around you.

If your life has been so disappointing that you think you can never recapture the wonder; if you consider yourself to be dry, boring and totally unimaginative or uncreative, remember the amazing creativity of God. He had a vision for this universe, and you and I were planned by Him.

If we belong to Him through faith in Jesus Christ, He has promised that we can have the mind that is in Christ Jesus (see 1 Corinthians 2:16; Philippians 2:5), and that the Holy Spirit will bring to our remembrance the Word of God and the ideas we need (see John 14:26). The mindset of the Creator of the world is ours for the taking. And if we are willing, He can help us to recapture the wonder and creative imagination of children.

FIVE

Respond like a Child, Part 2

Enthusiasm

Just before he died at the age of 93, Dr. Norman Vincent Peale finished and published his last book. Prior to that, Carl and I went to Fargo, North Dakota, to hear him speak. Afterward I asked Dr. Peale to give us a line on reversing the aging process.

He did not hesitate. "You're not old until you lose your enthusiasm," he declared. "Forget your age and get on with life."

On the way to the car Carl and I reflected on Dr. Peale's comment, and on the fact that we knew young and middle-aged people who were already old. In summing up Dr. Peale's philosophy, Carl came up with his own version: "Overlook the wrinkle and look for the twinkle!"

Enthusiasm: getting on with our lives regardless of ages and stages; looking for the twinkle in whatever life hands us. It is a simple philosophy, and maybe some people would call it unrealistic or Pollyanna-like. But since it is part of that childlike mentality Jesus has instructed us to adopt, let's look at it more closely.

Is It Scriptural?

Are we talking about some "positive-thinking, pull-your-self-up-by-your-bootstraps" kind of mush here? Or is enthusiasm for life a concept with a basis in Scripture?

Enthusiasm is actually defined by two Greek words that mean "God within." Joy is the undeniable sign of the presence of God—of God within. The Old Testament writer who said, "The joy of the Lord is your strength" (Nehemiah 8:10) was talking about joy with power, and so was Paul when he wrote about being "strengthened with all might, according to His glorious power, for all patience and longsuffering with joy" (Colossians 1:11). Joy with power certainly sounds like God within—like enthusiasm—to me!

I was not there at his race, but St. Paul was an old man who had fought a good fight and finished his course. I am sure he went across the finish line valiantly, with his head high. I do not believe God intends the elderly to stumble across the finish line of their invisible marathon, the unseen race of life. I do not know about you, but it gives me at 65 a renewed sense of "Let's get at it!" just to read about Paul's enthusiastic approach to life!

Florida Power came out this year with a bright yellow and red flyer boasting a new slogan—"You've got the power!" I think someone from their corporate headquarters must have visited our church, because we sing a chorus that starts, "We've got the power in the name of Jesus."

The Florida Power brochure reads, in part, "'You've got the power' may sound strange to you if you have always thought of your power company as the controlling source of electricity. After all, we generate the power, don't we? Of course that's true, but our relationship with you goes beyond the generation and delivery of power. 'You've got the power' empowers our employees. You've got the power and we hope you'll respond as often as possible to the programs and services we offer. Cash in on our energy upgrades."

Generating power? Energy upgrades? Sounds like a commercial for a revival center to me, or a *Reader's Digest* version of the book of Acts. We Christians do have the power, through Jesus Christ and the Holy Spirit, to live enthusiastic, joy-filled lives!

Where do children get their enthusiasm? Despite the unfortunate fact of original sin, human beings are still made in God's image. Children, therefore, do come with the inner attribute of enthusiasm—joy, power, God within. Most of them are born with the ability to see and hear more than most adults will ever take time to observe.

Part and parcel of children's enthusiasm is an enduring, God-given energy that is unexplainable. Have you noticed that they have two speeds, excited curiosity and exhausted sleep? Certainly some of children's energy and zest for life can be explained by the fact that their bodies are young and strong, but children have inner qualities of enthusiasm that young people and adults all too often dismiss as unsophisticated, immature or "uncool." The media and our jaded society have "done a number" on us in that respect. We should never squelch children's enthusiasm. Maybe instead we should capture it, bottle it and sell it!

I do believe that some people have to work at retaining or regaining their childlike enthusiasm, while others, by nature of their personalities or genes, are born with energetic, enthusiastic dispositions that last all their lives. One young woman in my circle of writing friends comes into the room like a white tornado. That is just her. Another woman, the mother of my prayer partner Dorothy Evans, was honored recently at the Kendall United Methodist Church in Miami for singing in the choir for 88 years! All of her children, grandchildren and great-grandchildren were there to celebrate her enthusiasm for music. That reminds me of the verse from Proverbs 31, "Her children rise up and call her blessed" (verse 28). How could you *not* love a woman with that kind of enthusiasm?

My editor, Jane Campbell, has inherited her vitality from her dad. He was an English and writing professor and an eternal optimist. He enjoyed being silly, and would pirouette across the living room floor just for fun. He never got old, though he died in 1991 at the age of 88.

Regaining—and Retaining—Our Enthusiasm

If we have the potential, through the living and written Word of God and through the power of the Holy Spirit, to live life with enthusiasm, how do we go about regaining and retaining that childlike quality so many of us lost years ago? How do we glide into old age with our enthusiasm intact?

We do it by studying enthusiasm as it manifests in children and by asking God to help us become like His precious little ones in this respect, too. Like the other childlike characteristics we are discussing in this book, enthusiasm has various hallmarks or traits. We will look at seven.

1. Enthusiasm Listens Eagerly to God

I believe we are born with ears on our hearts. Children listen to God. Perhaps because every child was God's idea in the first place, they are on His "wavelength."

The child Samuel thought Eli was calling him, but learned that it was God's voice instead. Samuel listened, then answered, apparently without hesitation, "Here I am; send me, I'm available." (See 1 Samuel 3.)

Chris and Deb Maxwell are young pastors of a church in Orlando, Florida. They have a little son, Aaron, who loves God.

One time they were on vacation, en route to a motel where they would stay near Disney World. They thought Aaron was asleep in the back seat but suddenly he popped up, stuck his little head between them and interrupted, "Dad, you need to see about Brother Cloud."

"Why do you say that, Aaron?" they asked. "We haven't been talking about Brother Cloud."

"My real Dad just told me that, in my heart," Aaron replied with confidence.

"What do you mean, your 'real Dad'?" Chris asked his son. "I am your real father. Where did you get that?"

"But God is my heavenly Father," Aaron explained, "and He was the one who told me you need to check on Brother Cloud."

As soon as the family was settled in their motel room, Chris called back home to learn that Mr. Cloud had just been taken to the hospital!

My friend and prayer partner Lois Mitchell recalls one night when her four-year-old granddaughter, Elizabeth, crawled up onto her lap and wanted to hear a bedtime story. Before Lois could make a suggestion, Elizabeth nudged like an adult philosopher: "About the man with the nails, Grandma." Minutes later Lois could tell that Elizabeth was inquiring seriously about the cross and the plan of salvation. At that young age, she confessed Jesus Christ as her Savior.

Remember when you were newly born of the Spirit, young in the things of God, enthusiastic for the milk of the Word with the hunger and thirst of a young baby for its mother's milk? Remember when you, too, listened eagerly to Him?

Go back to Him, your Source, and ask Him to help you listen eagerly once again.

2. Enthusiasm Believes Fervently in God and in Others

I wish I could make a trip today to a quaint little cemetery in Ellendale, North Dakota, to put a new epitaph over the old one on the gravestone of Roy Wead, former president of Trinity College. It would read like this:

> Roy Wead, president of Trinity College,
> He used a lot of adjectives.
> His imagination was questioned, but contagious,
> His energy unquenchable.
> His childlike enthusiasm could not be extinguished.
> He lived until he died.

I first recall Roy's influence on my life when he was superintendent of the Indiana district for our denomination. With his loving encouragement and enthusiasm he tricked my father, Glenn Perkins, into taking small, rundown churches with bad buildings, split congregations and low attendance.

"Pastor Perkins," he would say, "with God's help, you can make this church thrive again." Roy made my dad believe he could do it, and he did—nine times.

Roy became a major figure in my life again in 1971. Carl and I were planning to be married in June. Meanwhile, I was serving as housemother in Flower Hall at Central Bible College in Springfield, Missouri. Carl's wife had died and he was living in Mission Village, awaiting reappointment for an overseas mission.

Many of Carl's friends said our marriage could not work. I had never been to Bible school and had no experience in missions. (I had been only to heaven and Texas!) Carl was educated, while I majored in kids and minored in quarterhorses.

One day Roy Wead just happened to be passing through Springfield and called to ask, "Betty, could we have lunch today at noon?" While we ate he encouraged me, "Carl is a prince. I know you haven't known him for long, yet I've known your family since you were a child, and I see the two of you as 'partners for a purpose.' But please don't go overseas with children and stepchildren and honeymoon adjustments. I need a campus pastor and teacher at Trinity Bible College."

Roy's enthusiasm changed our plans. We were married and moved to Jamestown, North Dakota, where we found a house across from the little airport with a place for the children's horses and collie dogs.

Trinity College was housed in an old hospital, and during the years we knew him as president, Roy further stretched our imaginations by his belief in the teachers he hired, and by occasionally choosing staff members that we did not think "looked the part."

Roy's enthusiasm spurred us to believe in those North Dakota prairies and those hard-working people. North Dakota has two seasons, July and winter. When the temperature dipped to sixty degrees below zero, Roy and his wife, Rosa Mae, would take us for a ride in the country in their Mercury Marquis, pumping us up and praising those prairies.

"Look at that big sky!" Roy would say. "Where else can you see sturdy buffalo grazing grass between snowbanks in winter, and a thousand acres of sunflowers blooming like a yellow ocean in summer?" He always wore a lapel button that read, "N.D. keeps out the riff-raff," and as we drove along he would sing lustily, "Home, home on the range." Roy was right, those words did describe our new home.

Eight months after we arrived, Mr. Enthusiasm had a dream. The University of North Dakota was vacating its campus at Ellendale. Roy Wead came through our front door like a tall, white tornado. "This is a 'come as you are party,' all of you," he yelled. "I have something wonderful to show you!" April grabbed her cat, I went barefoot and Carl was still munching on his apple as we took off to look at the beautiful facility, complete with a 60,000-volume library, gymnasium, cafeteria, dormitories, an armory that could be used as a chapel and a gorgeous old three-story Victorian house for the president's residence.

Eventually Trinity bought the entire package for one American dollar. Two days later Israel and Anna Zimmerman decided they were too old to farm any longer, even as I was driving to Ellendale bolstered by Roy Wead's contagious enthusiasm that I could find a home for our family, horses and collie dogs. We bought the Zimmermans' comfortable two-story family home before it was even advertised. It came complete with a pond, a barn for the horses, a shed for the collie kennel and a two-car garage. It was located on a school bus route only two blocks from campus, so Carl could walk or ride his bike to work. It was the perfect place for our children to finish growing up among the real people, the hard-working people, the prairie people of the Dakotas.

Years later, after Roy Wead's death, we moved into the president's house. A few times during our 24-year-partnership, we have wondered if we would make it through marriage and career adjustments, but we have looked at each other and grinned: "We have to make it. We can't disappoint Roy Wead! He voted for us, he believed in us."

Roy's childlike enthusiasm was contagious in epidemic proportions; his cup ran over and it spilled onto us and onto the students. It was a step of faith to move to that north country after years of living near the beaches of Clearwater, Florida, but some of the most rewarding years of my life were spent there investing in people. Today everywhere that Carl and I travel we meet pastors, missionaries, singers, evangelists and writers from Trinity who were affected by Roy Wead and his legacy of enthusiasm.

What was Roy's source? The wellspring of his undying imagination and energy? He was a walking, talking Bible. He had hidden the Word in his heart since he was a child. Verses like "Whatever your hand finds to do, do it with your might" (Ecclesiastes 9:10) and, speaking of wisdom, "Those who love me [shall] inherit wealth, that I may fill their treasuries" (Proverbs 8:21) were the cornerstone of his life. He quoted Scripture almost unknowingly in casual conversation, writing, preaching or during a staff meeting. Scriptures surfaced and sped to his remembrance at the explicit opportune moment with enthusiasm and under the inspiration and anointing of the Holy Spirit.

3. Enthusiasm Is Creative

The story is told of a pastor's son who sat in the balcony throwing spitballs at bald heads below while Dad tried to concentrate on the message he was trying to deliver. Dad's dirty looks and shaking head were ineffective to stop the behavior, and after church Dad attempted to admonish his offspring.

"You just keep preaching, Dad," said the incorrigible boy, "and I'll keep them awake."

Yes, some of the boy's "antsy" behavior might have been due to a lack of interesting material in his father's sermons. But you have to give the lad credit: He was creative.

Enthusiasm stimulates motivation, and motivation is a creative force for productivity. In a story published by *Guideposts* magazine, Dr. Tony Ladd, a sports historian at Wheaton College, tells the story of his grandfather, Dr. James Naismith. An inventor and physician, Dr. Naismith joined the International YMCA Training School in Springfield, Massachusetts. There he found the age-old problem: bored young men in winter. The cold prevented outside activity and only a limited number of things could be done indoors. Yet Naismith felt it important to maintain the boys' interest in physical activities because he thought exercise was a perfect way to keep young men fit and on the straight and narrow path.

On December 21, 1891, the thirty-year-old Naismith received an inspiration for a game that almost became "boxball." He asked the YMCA janitor to secure two boxes that could be used for goals. The janitor could not find boxes, but produced a couple of peach baskets. Naismith improvised, mounted the baskets on the ten-foot-high gym railing and called it "basketball."

Within the hour the good doctor had created thirteen rules and started the new game with a soccer ball. The game spread rapidly. Naismith never patented the game or made any money from it. He simply relished the satisfaction of providing another vehicle to help in training minds, bodies and souls for the glory of God. Enthusiasm created basketball.

That kind of creativity has to start somewhere, and often it starts in children's imaginations. Don't squelch young'uns when they stretch their imaginations a bit. I seriously believe that faith is sanctified imagination.

I heard a speaker tell about his little son, who would not carry out the waste paper at dusk one evening because he thought there was a bear in the back yard. His father argued that it was just a dog, and then lectured the child for stretching the truth.

"That's a form of lying," he scolded, and told the little guy to go to his room and talk to God about it.

When the child came out of his room later he told his daddy, "God told me, 'You're right, it was a bear.'"

I realize enthusiasm has to be taken in moderation, but it does not hurt for adults or children to "let go" in raucous laughter and creative imagination. Don't squelch children as long as they are not hurting anybody. Life will get serious enough, soon enough. The child who is allowed to use that creative imagination in healthy ways will grow to be an adult who uses it enthusiastically and appropriately.

4. Enthusiasm Stimulates Perseverance

I spoke at a nurses' convention at the medical center in Tupelo, Mississippi. Shortly after I was there one of the nurses mailed me a story illustrating that adults are "quick quitters," while children do not give up easily when they want something badly.

A little boy pestered his parents day in and day out to buy him a watch. They put him off every way they could. Finally he drove them to the breaking point.

"I don't want to hear another word about a watch," the father said firmly. And for over a week the lad complied.

Every Sunday afternoon this family sat together for family devotions. Each child was required to memorize and recite a Scripture verse he or she had learned that week. On this particular Sunday, after every other family member had quoted a verse, it was the little boy's turn. He had chosen well. Looking up with a very solemn face, he quoted his verse perfectly—and embellished it: "Watch and pray, that ye enter not into temptation. What I say unto you, I say unto all, Watch, and Jesus said, 'Again I say unto you, Watch'" (see Matthew 26:41, KJV). The lad's cunning persistence paid off. He got his watch.

History is full of things and events that "couldn't be done," but childlike enthusiasm, whether found in a body large or small, spurred on the human spirit. Neither riches, great brains nor vast opportunity accomplished the goals of John Tyndale, the Wright brothers, Charles Lindbergh, Martin Luther King or Susan B. Anthony. They had enthusiasm's "staying power"—perseverance.

5. Enthusiasm Has a Great Sense of Humor

A cousin to the word *enthusiasm* is the word *mirth*. It means "merry, with gladness, accompanied by laughter, characterized by joy and manifested by high spirits."

The book of Proverbs talks about humor. One of its most famous pieces of advice is that "a merry heart does good, like medicine" (Proverbs 17:22).

Lindy Platten-Jarvis lives in Yew Tree Cottage, Felthorpe, Norwich, Norfolk, England. For her new book, titled *God Whistles, God Sings*, she has researched and dug out the humor in stories in the Bible.

Billy Crystal, star of the movie *City Slickers*, has said, "Laugh at yourself. It's all a part of healing. . . . All very unpredictable and magical in that electrochemical way. That's what is so great about a laugh; it's this chemical reaction in your body that makes you silly for a couple of seconds. You just can't express yourself except in this sound. It's an 'infantlike' reaction."

Crystal is right. The chuckle of a baby is a healing balm akin to the healing virtue of the Christ who made, respected and urged us to become like little ones.

Little children can laugh at their own silliness. Even more, they can laugh at ours. And sometimes they save our sanity by providing opportunities for us to laugh (without letting on) at them.

My Aunt Gwendolyn is the youngest great-grandmother I have ever known. Her pride, joy and entertainment are her two little great-granddaughters, Maggie and Amanda.

One day when Maggie was about seven, she spent all day bossing her little sister, and even her great-grandmother, around. Disgusted at her behavior, her father asked, "Maggie, who died and left you in charge?"

Without missing a beat, Maggie pointed to the picture of her late grandmother, Barbara, sitting on the hutch. "She, Barbara, did," she retorted.

Another Saturday when Aunt Gwendolyn was babysitting the girls, they were exceptionally rowdy. Exhausted, she finally raised her voice to ask, "Why don't you two just be normal?"

"What's normal, Nana?" asked little Amanda.

A man once asked a psychologist, "What is the most important thing my son can get from me?"

The doctor replied, "A sense of humor."

"Why?" asked the surprised father.

"Because humor is the shock absorber of life," the psychologist explained. "It helps us take life's blows. Humor allows us to step out of the moment, look at it and sum it up with no great reverence. It is a gift nature gives the mature intellect."

President John F. Kennedy had a low-key sense of humor that was amazing. A newscaster once asked him, "How did you become a war hero?"

Kennedy replied, "It was easy; they sank my boat."

Someone gave me a cup imprinted, "Laugh at yourself before others have a chance to laugh at you. Don't take life so seriously; you're never going to get out of here alive. If you're going to laugh, laugh out loud. Vibrate your system; it's a tonic that insures good health."

A person is rarely good at anything they do not have a little fun doing. It is a sign that the enthusiasm has leaked out. In the movie *Little Big League* an eleven-year-old boy inherits the Minnesota Twins baseball club. He tells the players, "You've quit having a good time at your games." Why does humor affect our performance? Because it is contagious: "And Sarah said, 'God has made me laugh, so that all who hear will laugh with me'" (Genesis 21:6).

I believe you can survive with a sense of humor, a good job and childlike faith in God. I sat at the organ bench to play for my mother-in-law's funeral, but try as I might I could produce no sound. The funeral director was frantic. Two minutes before the service, after we had tried everything we could think of, the custodian, who knew absolutely nothing about music or organs, plugged the instrument in.

Do you feel unplugged? Look at the kids. Plug into God's mirth.

6. Enthusiasm Gives Generously

Have you noticed that children give with genuine enthusiasm?

When our youngest daughter was perhaps three, our family sat in a church where we had gone to hear a youth choir sing. At mid-concert, the pastor asked us to close our eyes. While he prayed, we were to ask the Lord what He wanted us to give to keep this worthy group going. After the prayer, I looked into my billfold. It was "dry"; there was nothing in it. Yet I knew I had had seven dollars before we left home.

When the offering bag passed me, I smiled and handed it on to my daughter. She put her doubled-up fist deep into the bag. Was she pretending? Did she have money of her own with her?

After we returned home I learned that while I had my eyes closed, praying what God would have me give, she had thought she heard from the Lord and emptied my billfold!

Children love to give. I taught second- and third-graders in Sunday school for several years. Every week I would ask my husband to give me a lot of change so I could give every child something to put into the offering during "big church," morning worship. This was my "on hand" way of teaching the joy of giving. Watching my students out of the corner of my eye, I saw that they loved it.

I never told the parents what I was doing, but my secret got out. One week the Sunday school superintendent, Jesse Mullins, invited several children up front and asked them, "What do you like best about church?"

"Putting money in the offering," two children replied enthusiastically.

"Do you like your teacher?" Jesse went on.

"Yes," another child answered quickly. "She gives us the money to put in the offering."

My niece Shanda is working while attending college. On her last visit here, I shared this part of my book. She in turn shared a secret concept, an anonymous habit. She gives all her change into the offering wherever she is, when any offering is taken. In time it amounts to a sizable contribution for a person with a small income.

My grandmother Mom Perky taught me, "If you are depressed, give something away." It cures; it works every time.

One Christmas season I was helping with a telethon. One of the volunteers was named Pearl.

"If my name were Pearl," I remarked jokingly, "I would wear a pearl necklace, pearl earrings, pearl everything. If my name were Ruby, I would wear rubies and adopt my own logo."

"I don't have anything pearl, but I would like to do that," Pearl replied. "It sounds like fun, but I never thought of it."

When I left for the airport that day, I slipped my cheap, synthetic pearl ring onto her finger and said, as befitted the season, "Merry Christmas!"

A few days later, when we opened our gifts around the tree, one present for me was a velvet box from Carl David, our son. In it were a pearl necklace, a pearl bracelet and a pearl keyring in the shape of a heart.

"God loves a cheerful giver," says Paul in 2 Corinthians 9:7, and "Give, and it will be given to you" (Luke 6:38). Those Scriptures surely came true for me!

Cheerful, enthusiastic, childlike giving is a two-way street. When Karen Siddle visited me, I sent a bag of pecans home with her for her mother to use in baking for the holidays. To my surprise, shortly afterward I received an enormous box of pecans from my friend Madge Stack in Meridian, Mississippi!

My sister-in-law Sharon loves cashew nuts. One year for a fun birthday gift, I sent her a small jar of cashews. At Christmas that year I got a large tin of cashews from our neighbors, the Stambaughs.

The little boy in the Bible gave his lunch, all five loaves and two fishes. God multiplied them, offering a magical miracle for a lad to witness. Can you believe the mathematics of that embarrassing abundance? The disciples collected twelve baskets of leftovers (see John 6)!

Millie Hansen was enthusiastically childlike in her faith and giving. She asked her pastors to pray for the pain in her shoulder and back. God gave her an extra bonus, another perk for believing: Not only did He get rid of the pain, but her blind eyes were healed, too. Now Millie has bought a car and is driving people to church in exchange for the years that others drove her.

7. Enthusiasm Takes Risks

My youngest brother, Gary, broke both arms just a few weeks apart. He got carried away with enthusiasm when he saw the Ringling Brothers Circus. He did not know he could not walk on the clothesline as the Great Wallenda family walked the tightrope!

Try not to squelch your childlike enthusiasm. Stretch yourself. Do something you are not comfortable with. Exercise risk. Kids receive miracles because they are enthusiastic and do not know they "cannot" happen.

Peter would never have known he could walk on the water to the Lord, unless he tried. Peter and the disciples had a unique sense of enthusiasm. Read about it in John 21:7: If you want to catch 153 fish, fish naked. Peter did!

A Caution

Catherine Marshall shared with me a valuable lesson about enthusiasm. I want to pass it on.

Catherine coached me, "Share your faith with enthusiasm, but don't share your writing ideas, and don't expect people to be enthusiastic about the things God reveals to you. Each person you tell your concept or project to can punch a hole of unbelief in the pipeline. By the time it gets to the end, like a waterline its fervor has leaked out, lost its pressure.

"Mary must have been enthusiastic about carrying a child for the Holy Spirit," Catherine went on, "but she kept those things in her heart until Jesus was born for fear of relief robbing the joy."

Wise words. Enthusiasm is a facet of being childlike, but it must be guarded with maturity and moderation.

Abundant Life

The simplicity of enthusiasm, its childlikeness, is refreshing in our complex society. "There is more to life than increasing its speed," wrote Mahatma Gandhi. Enthusiasm is part of the "more," the abundant life that Jesus came to bring us (see John 10:10).

As we will discuss in the next chapter, children capture that abundant life by being enthusiastic in their love, as well. If only we could be like them! When they fall six times, they get up seven. How do they do it?

SiX

Love like a Child

The Transforming Power of Caring

L et me do it, Mommy, let me do it. I can reach it, I can reach it."

A writer always has a nose for a story, so I could not resist stepping back to watch as little Johnathan stretched to reach the fourth-row box on the Post Office wall. Inserting the key, he exulted, "I did it!" He was so enthusiastic, so small, but he had finally grown tall enough to "deliver the mail."

Thinking the little drama was over, I was ready to go about my own business when I saw the little fellow turn and call out to a crotchety, frowning old woman standing nearby.

"Morning, Ms. Martha. Did you get any mail? I got the mail by myself. I'm getting taller and taller."

The woman's stony face showed no response whatsoever; she did not even mumble a word in reply to the little guy before she left the building. In an attempt to soothe his disappointment, his young mother, Winona, offered, "Maybe she has a sore throat and can't talk right now, or she may be going deaf. Some old people can't hear too well."

"Nice try, Mom!" I winked at her. We both knew the old woman talked to no one, trusted no one and was convinced that everyone was out to gyp her. Crystal Beach is a small, peaceful fishing village, and we found it hard to believe that a person could remain so callous in its warm and caring environment.

Winona called me the following week with an amazing report. "When we got to the car that day, my son was touched with such caring tenderness. 'Mommy,' he mused, 'Ms. Martha keeps opening her box, but she never, never gets any mail. I want to stop at Eckerd's Drugstore and buy her a real pretty Valentine card.'

"We did," Winona continued. "I was so moved as the little guy reached deep into his pocket to buy the card for 'the witch' [what many called her]. He lacked twelve cents, which I supplied. Back home he printed his name, 'Johnathan,' with his best effort, then went the second mile and scrawled, 'I Love You.'

"In my mind's eye," Winona admitted, "I could just see her tear it up or ignore it. I thought she might not even bother to open the card he so tenderly selected."

But upon receiving the card three days later, the old woman called Winona. She was weeping hoarsely as she said, "I have not gotten a Valentine since I was in the seventh grade when we had to bring one for a grab-bag Valentine exchange."

The transforming power of Johnathan's childlike love has been evident ever since. Ms. Martha speaks to citizens of our community, showed up for Christmas caroling in the park and went to church on Christmas Sunday. We had prayed a long time for this cold, miserly, hard heart. It is good to pray. God can work miracles, but He may require that we, like Johnathan, do some homework. Yes, a little child shall lead them.

One Essential Element

Talk about simplicity! The Christian life has one simple, essential element—love. In his famous chapter on love (1 Corinthians 13) Paul comments that if we have gifts of service, articulate speech and self-sacrifice—all great gifts!—but do not have love, we are nothing. He then goes on to describe the kind of love that needs to characterize the Christian:

> Love suffers long and is kind; love does not envy; love does not parade itself, is not puffed up; does not behave rudely, does not seek its own, is not provoked, thinks no evil; does not rejoice in iniquity, but rejoices in the truth; bears all things, believes all things, hopes all things, endures all things. Love never fails.
>
> verses 4–8

Loving like a child means living out this description of love in our daily lives, something we can do only through the power of the Holy Spirit.

One Christmas Eve I was sitting in the Memphis airport, halfway home, waiting for the last leg of my flight into Tampa. Everyone was restless and flights were late. Near my seat, the mother of a little African-American boy was riding him for everything he did or said. When he leaned against the bar across the plate glass window to watch the planes in the early night light, she said, "If you dust that rod one more time—"

"I'm not dusting it, I just leaned to see the plane way up there," he interrupted.

"Now that you have disputed my word, you will be punished not one day, but three," his mama declared.

The little fellow looked as though a light went out of his insides.

I wanted to cheer him up. He looked at my big, shiny, black patent purse that is a clock, and said, "I wish my mother had one of those."

"Tell your daddy to get her one for Christmas," I suggested.

"We don't celebrate Christmas," he reported. "Our religion don't let us."

No wonder his mother was such a grouch. No Christmas. No Christ. I was nearing my 65th birthday and do not think the child inside of me even at this age could function and survive without Christmas, the Christ Child, trees and lights.

As these thoughts were going through my mind, another little boy spoke up and said, "My ancestors killed the man who said he was the Son of God, and you still celebrate Christmas." I have never felt such compassion for two children as I did for those two little boys. I wanted to steal them, take them home and let them celebrate Christmas.

I got on my homeward flight and tried to take a nap, but I could not fall asleep, so I opened the *Sky* magazine and found an article that was right on target for this chapter: "If You Care Enough." The author stated that cynics suggest people do not care as much as they once did. Caring is a necessary ingredient that unites families and personal relationships, guarantees friendships and (this even applies to big business!) quality work.

Simply put, there is a quality of caring that is transforming. It will promote or protect oneself or another. Without it, emotional and physical growth suffer. With it, one can move mountains.

Those thoughts expressed in a secular magazine were absolutely true, yet how much more effective love and caring are when they are inspired by and communicated with the power of the Holy Spirit! How I wished that mother in the airport had known the transforming love of Jesus so she could have shared it in the way she dealt with her children!

How to Love like a Child

As I have observed children, both over the years and in preparation for this book, I have learned that living out the childlike love described in 1 Corinthians 13 requires activating our wills to take at least seven steps. Let's look at these steps on the following pages.

Step 1: Loving like a Child Requires Sensitivity to Need

I believe children, unless squelched, come standard-equipped with special "vibes," and their loving vibrations seem to register when another human being has need of a cheerleader, of someone to be in his or her corner. Somehow children often know just when we need the transforming power of caring in our lives.

Tissy, the owner of the boutique where I work, loves children. She keeps a basket of toys available for the little guys to play with while their mothers are in the dressing room.

One Saturday a young mother of three came in, apologizing for having to bring her children along. The two smallest children played on the floor with the toys, but the five-year-old went out to the ramp by the side door. I watched closely, but he was safe, playing with the rocks along the flower bed.

Suddenly he came through the door on "fast forward," as most boys do at the age of five. (I had four brothers. I believe anything you tell me about boys, even before you begin!)

"Do you have a restroom?" he asked.

"We have two," I replied, "and I'm going to let you use the prettiest one." It also was the closest, since it was obvious he was in a hurry.

"Thank you," he said, and hurried back outside. He returned right away and, with a sheepish grin, went into the bathroom, carrying something in his hand.

A horrible thought came into my mind. We have toads that leap around outside our door. I do not like toads; they are not ugly, they are just toads. Would he put one in the lavatory? Or—oh no—not the stool!

After a bit the little boy came out and said to me, "Shut your eyes, and hold out your hand. I washed something pretty and clean just for you." Oh no, not a toad. . . . I cringed, but I cooperated. I love kids—and I wanted his mother to buy something.

Gently the little boy laid in my hand a pretty white rock about the size of a quarter. "Look," he said. "It's got silver and diamonds inside."

How his gift touched me! I was all alone that particular week. My nephew had had a serious wreck and was unconscious in University Hospital in Jacksonville; we had had a death in our family; and my husband was fulfilling a speaking engagement in India. I needed that child's transforming power of caring.

James Dobson told on his radio program about young parents who were concerned when their little girl arrived late for dinner.

"Where were you?" the daddy inquired.

The little girl explained that she had stopped by to visit a couple whose small daughter had died recently.

"What did you say to them?" the mother asked.

"Nothing," said the little girl. "I just crawled up on the mother's lap and cried with her."

Sometimes we give such shallow, canned answers to sorrow's questions. Paul said, "Weep with those who weep" (Romans 12:15). Life is tough. Life is not fair. Sometimes tears are uncontrollable.

But, you say, only babies cry. Not so. Jesus cried. I can recall at least three places in which the Bible tells us that

He wept. Once He cried over Jerusalem, because He had come to the inhabitants of that beloved city, but they had rejected Him. He was their hope, but they did not recognize who He really was (see Luke 13:34). Jesus also cried with Mary and Martha when their brother and His friend, Lazarus, died (John 11:35). And Jesus cried in prayer at Gethsemane before He went to the cross, cried out to the Father for your sins and mine, for your sickness and mine (Matthew 26).

As someone once said, "'Tis better heart without words, than words without heart."

Miriam Blohm has been in charge of the Crystal Beach Post Office for several years. One day I learned in casual conversation that her husband, Roger's, elderly, infirm mother has come to live in their home. In addition, Miriam and Roger's two-year-old granddaughter, Annalee, spends a great deal of time at their house.

One day Miriam watched, unnoticed, while Roger's mother struggled, trying to reach for her walker so she could get across the room to her bed. Little Annalee toddled over and, without saying a word, slowly pushed the walker nearer to her great-grandmother's outstretched hands. When Great-Grandma finally reached the bed, tiny Annalee tucked a blanket around her and said tenderly, "Now lie down."

Two tiny hands, three tiny words, but what a wealth of sensitivity they shared!

Ken House is the founder of "Care Ministry." Our church took Care Ministry's training, taught by Fred Kropp. He emphasized that people usually come to church because they have needs or are lonely. If seven people do not show themselves personally concerned about those needs and lonely feelings within six weeks, the visitors (or maybe even regular attendees) are "out of there."

God has supplied so many of our needs that we have become complacent in our comfort zones, insensitive to the needs of those around us. Sensitivity to need comes easily for children, but we adults may need to ask the Holy Spirit to help us relearn it.

Step 2: Loving like a Child Requires a Sense of Appreciation

Last year on Mother's Day I read in a newspaper a true story that illustrates a child's sense of appreciation. It seems that a little boy went into a dress shop and told the sales clerk, "I want to buy a dress for Mommy for Mother's Day."

"What size is she?" the clerk asked.

"Just right!" he answered knowingly. The clerk helped him to choose a dress in the size she assumed he meant and, since his dad had not given him quite enough money to pay for it, gave it to him for a "bargain" price.

On the Monday after Mother's Day, a young woman weighing about 285 pounds walked into the store to exchange the lovely size ten dress for one in her "just right" size!

It did not matter to that little boy how big or how small his mother was. He appreciated her for who she was, and wanted to let her know!

I thrive on appreciation. One day I was having a hard time unwinding and then jumping into housework and the mountain of mail waiting for me after my return home from a trip involving a three-hour time change. But was I ever glad I opened the mail for, like magic, there was a letter of appreciation! It read,

Dearest Betty,

Hello! My name is Catherine Hinchcliff. I'm 12 years old and in the 6th grade. I came with my mother, Nancy, to hear you speak at a church between Skapoose and St. Helen's, Oregon. Thank you for the angel pictures like the ones in your book *Angels Watching Over Me*. You have made me realize I should pray more than just for meals and bedtime.

My little brother Mikey was born with De George Syndrome and two holes in his heart. He has a hard time sleeping sometimes. He came into my room and I got him a glass of water, then he went to my sister's room, then came back to mine. Our mom came into our room and prayed for us a prayer that was so wonderful. We instantly went to sleep, honestly it was the best night's sleep I had in days.

You said it in your speech, and it is true. I tell you, never underestimate the power of prayer!

Thanks for coming to Oregon.

> In Christian love,
> Catherine Hinchcliff

That day I was a good example of the saying, "I was put on this earth to accomplish a certain number of things, but right now I'm running so far behind, I'll probably never get to die." I was tired, but I was strengthened, cheered and spurred on by the appreciation of a twelve-year-old I had never met who wrote a letter. I do not need much, but I can survive, even thrive, on appreciation.

Step 3: Loving like a Child Requires Spontaneous Generosity

My friend Pam Peck teaches preschoolers in Odessa, Florida. The last day of the semester she was stressed out from the activities of the past weeks, and especially from the effort of putting on a play for her students' parents the previous evening.

As the children were leaving the classroom, saying their goodbyes until the next year, Pam felt her adrenaline starting to wane. Then four-year-old Jennifer handed her an envelope, standing still to watch while she opened it. Big letters on the front read *Important*. Inside on the card was a string of illegible letters—and 36 pennies.

"What does your message say?" Pam asked Jennifer.

"I forgot," she answered, but explained that the 36 pennies were from her savings.

"Teacher," said Jennifer, "you can buy something very nice for yourself with it."

Spontaneous generosity, the transforming power of caring from a small pupil to a very tired young teacher, worked its restorative magic again.

In my own life the spontaneous love of a child has been my key to survival on more than one occasion. When I travel, I carry two Mother's Day cards and a letter in my briefcase. These are my "uppers."

The letter came from Brenda, my oldest daughter, while she was at youth camp when she was thirteen. My husband and her father had died the summer before.

Dear Mother,
   We're going to make it. Thanks for all you do for me. I love you very much.

                                                    Brenda

One of the Mother's Day cards came from five-year-old April. She made it out of pink construction paper and scrawled with a crayon, "To the Best Mother in The World. xxxxxooooo April Dawn."

The other card was from Connie. When she was twelve, her mother died. I married her dad, Carl Malz, after Connie introduced us. Inside her card was this message:

I'm glad you happened to me. Thanks for being there when I need you and when I come home off the school bus.
                                                    Love, Connie

These tokens of my children's spontaneous generosity sustain me, keep me going. Whenever I feel a little down, I look at them, touch them, read them again. Sometimes they are the difference between hope and despair when things get rough. I would give you my old classic MGA convertible or my house, but I would not part with these three hand-written treasures.

We adults must recapture a child's spontaneous generosity, and with it the ability to transform others' days by our caring.

Step 4: Loving like a Child Requires Humility

Didn't we talk about humility in the last chapter? you're wondering. Yes, but there is no getting away from this all-important quality of childlikeness. It is not only part of a child's perspective; it is a factor in how a child loves. And we need to keep humility in focus because we grown-ups forget all too easily to cultivate it.

As a young man the great King Saul was head and shoulders taller than any man in his nation, yet humble before God like a child. As long as he remained meek, God used Saul to rule the great nation of Israel.

But, as happens with so many adults who gain power, status or money, Saul's childlike, humble love leaked out. In his case, jealousy caused the leak. Saul loved David, the shepherd singer, whose harp and songs eased Saul's depression. But when the nation of Israel discovered David and made him the object of their admiration and love, Saul's love for David—a love that had actually transformed David into a leader in the first place!—was canceled out by jealousy.

Saul's downhill slide from great humility to weak pride brought sorrow and disaster to himself, his family and his nation. "When you were little in your own eyes, were you not head of the tribes of Israel?" Samuel asked Saul. ". . . Why then did you not obey the voice of the Lord? . . . You have rejected the word of the Lord, and the Lord has rejected you from being king over Israel" (1 Samuel 15:17, 19, 26). Samuel anointed David as the king who would replace Saul, but instead of cooperating with God's plan with penitent humility and grace, Saul made it necessary for David to flee for his life. At one point David could have killed Saul, but his childlike love for Saul's honored position restrained him.

You would think David would have learned from Saul's example, but after he became king he took God for granted and sinned. God frowns on pride and arrogance, and David was punished. He did regain much of his childlike, humble love, for God and for people, and finished his reign with honor.

Oh, that men and women would remain humble in their ability to love!

George Fox was born in England in 1624. At the age of eleven, just a child, he surrendered his heart to the Lord and began to pursue the course in humility that God would use to enable him to win souls for the Kingdom to come.

One day, seeking advice about his calling from a clergyman, young George accidentally stepped on the man's flower bed. The clergyman flew into a rage. At that point George realized breeding and education from Oxford and Cambridge did not necessarily qualify a man to be a loving minister of Jesus Christ.

This incident so wounded George Fox's spirit that he determined to remain humble like a child, seeking his guidance from the Bible. He began preaching with limited education. He walked barefoot into crowded markets and streets with unquenchable love for lost souls. His prayers against superstition, intolerance and the deadness of the formal, institutional Church changed God's Kingdom in England, Ireland, Scotland, the West Indies and North America. The name *Quaker* was attached to Fox and his followers, because sinners who came to scoff would shake and quake and stay to pray.

George Fox, a man with scarcely any worldly advantages but with humble, childlike love and faith, influenced the then-known world for God and was buried beside Susanna Wesley and Isaac Watts.

I flew into St. Louis a few years ago to speak at a church with a humble, unpretentious name: The Sheep Shed. Somewhat to my surprise it was a sizable church, filled with exciting people. The reason for the name? The pastor explained: "When two people make love, babies are born. Sheep must love each other to produce lambs."

Does our childlike, humble love produce lambs for the Kingdom of God?

Step 5: Loving like a Child Requires Intercession

It has been said, "You think your book bag is the heaviest until you pick up someone else's by mistake." When Jesus was on earth, He gravitated toward need. We must follow His example. Children and grown-ups need the transforming power of our loving intercession, our prayers for the needs of others, as though they were our very own needs.

Children are not afraid to pray earnestly for the needs of others. Our children's church director tells how little Mike read out loud from his small New Testament, "My heart is fixed, O God, my heart is fixed" (Psalm 57:7, KJV). Then he read, "His heart is fixed" (Psalm 112:7, KJV). He asked the children around him, "Please pray for my Uncle Bert's heart attack. Ask Jesus to fix his heart."

Who could tell Mike he had misinterpreted a Scripture that literally meant that David had his heart slanted, or inclined, toward God? Strangely enough, Uncle Bert was back to work in less than a week—another "unexplainable" to adults.

Eunice Roberts loves children, and takes literally Luke 18:16, "Let the little children come to Me, and do not forbid [hinder] them." Eunice runs a state-approved daycare home for ten small children. She believes that when you take care of God's little ones, even angels come to assist you.

One morning Eunice awakened early, feeling something was wrong. She prayed for the safety of the little people and the home, and things went well. But when at the day's end she started backing her car out of the drive, she ran over something. It was Gina, the eighteen-month-old child who lived next door.

"I did not panic, but felt that I was a robot and someone had punched the 'super-calm' button," she remembers. She backed off the child's body and got out of the car. Someone lifted the child and placed her little body in Eunice Roberts' arms. She feels it was an unseen angel, since she does not recall picking Gina up and walking, as she did, toward the kitchen window, where Gina's mother had seen the accident happen.

There were ugly, black tire-tread marks on both of Gina's little arms from her shoulders down, but Gina looked up at Eunice and asked to be put down. Then she ran off to play. It was impossible! Gina's dad came running from the back yard exclaiming, "It's a miracle!" The next day Gina had no bruise marks on her.

God rewards Eunice's kind of praying. Volunteer to be a prayer intercessor as one way to live out childlike love in your life.

Step 6: Loving like a Child Requires Caring Involvement

Caring involvement is active. It does not hang back, afraid. Caring involvement jumps in at the nudge of the Holy Spirit and makes a difference.

Jesus said, "By this shall all men know that ye are my disciples, if ye have love one to another" (John 13:35, KJV). Not, "love *for* another." You can have a gift *for* a person, but unless you get it *to* them, they will never know it, will never be blessed, benefited and loved by it. Having love *for*, but not *to*, is like going Christmas shopping but never wrapping or sending the gifts you purchased. To love in words and not in deeds is like a garden full of weeds.

Dr. Gail Melson, professor of child development and family studies at Purdue University, implies that we can learn caring involvement from children. "Look at children in a waiting room or grocery store," she says. "You will see the perfect example of caring involvement." Dr. Melson tells of positioning an eight-month-old infant on the floor of a playroom. The mother was told to observe but not interact as 71 other children were brought into the room. The children all looked at the baby. One-third of them came close by, smiled and offered the baby a toy. Half of them got down face-to-face with the infant and most of them touched him.

You may receive nudges from the Holy Spirit toward many kinds of caring involvement. An elementary school teacher told me about the children in her class in northern Wisconsin, most of whom were from alcoholic families and single-parent situations. Many of them had never seen or heard the flush of an indoor toilet. Often they were filled with fear and confusion when they arrived at school.

Like many of his classmates, one little six-year-old rode the bus a long distance each day, coming in from a remote Indian village. He was unable to print his name, and the young teacher told me how she spent long hours trying to help him learn. Her loving perseverance paid off, and he did it—he wrote his name. Light broke through as he realized that he was capable, just like the other children. He could do it.

Excited, the teacher grabbed the little guy and hugged him. The following morning when he got off the school bus he tugged shyly at her skirt. "Teacher, if I do that again, will you do that again?" She asked him to explain. He promised to print his name again if she would hug him. Inquiring, she learned that no one had ever hugged him before. The transforming power of caring!

Maybe you are supposed to write letters to people you suspect get very little mail. They could even be your parents! I average 32 pieces of mail each day from readers of my books. I enjoy those letters, although before I read them, I quickly sort through every envelope, straining my eyes to see the small handwriting that indicates my daughters' return addresses.

The Bible mentions a ministry of "helps," to which is attached great reward (see 1 Corinthians 12:28). It also talks about exhorting, or encouraging, others (see Romans 12). Be a balcony person; cheer someone on. Never withhold love where it can transform another. Give your caring involvement freely, as children do.

Even a person in a coma responds to genuine caring involvement. Looking back several years to my 44 comatose days before death and my wonderful resurrection experience, I remember being unable to respond. But I could hear and understand, and I was very sensitive to, very aware of, the people in my hospital room.

One day an ordinary man, Art Lindsey from Toad Hop, Indiana, walked into my room. Even though he was aware that I did not like him personally, he opened his Bible and read Psalm 107:20, "He sent forth his word, and healed them." The transforming power of caring, coupled with the power of the Word, offered me hope. Days later I saw ivory letters pulsating toward my hospital bed: "I am the resurrection and the life; he that believeth in Me, though he were dead, yet shall he live" (John 11:25, KJV). I sat up, and have lived thirty years since then. My prejudice against Art was healed and I learned to love and invest in people.

Art Lindsey is still taking his simple, childlike love to prisoners. He has received many citations from governors for this ministry, and has a weekly radio broadcast called "Gospel Light," declaring God's love. Love works. The Word and caring transform.

"Isn't prayer caring involvement?" you ask. Yes, prayer does require an act of the will, an action toward another person. But sometimes God asks us to do more. He does the miraculous, but many times He uses us. I meet people who are pretty but not practical, fancy but not functional. Prayer works, but sometimes God gives people the insight to initiate solutions.

An elderly woman with a 35-year-old retarded daughter kept calling me long-distance to say, "Pray for my daughter; she is not well. She is depressed and very dizzy." Sometimes she called four times a day, and I would pray, talk with and encourage her.

Finally one day I felt led to call a minister in her city and ask him to call on the mother and daughter. He learned that the daughter was dizzy because the elderly mother was accidentally overdosing her with Valium.

Loving like a child requires more than good feelings. Sometimes it requires caring involvement beyond prayer. And obedience is more fun than sacrifice!

Step 7: Loving like a Child Requires Commitment

"I don't want your money, I want my Daddy!"

The scream came from a little girl in our neighborhood whose parents were separated. At the end of his weekly visiting privileges the father had kissed her goodbye and given her ten dollars.

This child represents so many whose lives have been torn apart because their parents' love was not childlike enough to include lifelong, "no-matter-what" commitment. Children are incredibly faithful in their commitments to the people they love; witness the stubborn love of so many children for their abusive parents. How devastating it is when their childlike love is not returned, and even worse, tossed aside.

I get so many letters from people with troubled marriages. These injuries are not inflicted by one disappointment. They result from actions and words that pile up to resemble the Chinese torture called "the death of a thousand cuts." The tormentor ties up the victim and inflicts a few tiny cuts from a razor blade every day, until the victim dies slowly, oozing to death.

Many people—even Christians—do this to their mates, their children, their parents, their friends.

Jesus said to some lukewarm Christians, "I have this against you, that you have left your first love. . . . Repent and do the first works [things you did at first]" (Revelation 2:4–5). I know He was talking about their love for God, but His words apply to our earthly loves as well.

Commitment comes in all shapes and sizes, but it is an essential companion to caring involvement. Without it, caring involvement is hollow, shallow. Without it, our attempts at caring involvement become like "sounding brass" or "a clanging cymbal" (see 1 Corinthians 13:1).

So refresh your mind: Go back to the day when you first confessed Jesus as Savior and Lord. Remember the Source of your first dedication. Then look at your wedding pictures. Renew your love and your vows. Study those photo albums and strengthen your family connections. Look through the church directory and decide to forgive and recommit to your fellow members of the Body of Christ today. Take a look at your checkbook: Have you been putting your money (commitment) where your mouth is?

Love Is a Daily Thing

Every human being needs love and caring on a daily basis in order to survive. Frances Pulley, a seventy-year-old mother from Paducah, Kentucky, sent me her original poem entitled "Everyday Love."

> Everyday love like everyday clothes fits best,
>   more comfortable. . . .
> Bibbed overalls, blue denim shirts, hand-me-downs
>   to my sister and me,
> That's all we had ever known.

Mrs. Pulley goes on telling that her mother was a widow left with eight children. She would get out the old number-two washtub and a bar of soap to scrub the clothes. After the last rinse, the children got their scrub.

> Mother sewed and every stitch in those faded, mended
>   clothes was how she told her love.
> Everyday clothes with everyday love, more comfortable
>   than Sunday dress.
> Oh yes, for the Sabbath Day, with one outfit we had
>   been blessed.
> But the old, faded, patched clothes we would put back
>   on, to play in the fields and hollows and stay
>   there 'till dark.
> Thanks to my sons and daughter, today I wear good, better
>   and best, you see,
>   but those everyday clothes with Mama's everyday
>   love
> Still live in my memories.

I like it; I believe it. Mrs. Pulley's thoughts echo the joy of simplicity to be found in childlike love, a joy I experienced as a child growing up in a household of pastor's children. We did not have much, but we had love and security. We did not know we were not rich; we had a rich heritage.

We can share the transforming power of childlike love and caring with children young and old, large and small, our own or the children of others. An old song is titled "I Want to Spend My Life Mending Broken People." I know thirty-year-olds who are standing dead, void of God's love so readily available to them, and empty of natural love because they cannot give or receive.

Oh, the magnitude of Jesus' simple concept: Love God first, then love people. Are you missing the boat? You may be trying too hard. Let God give His love through you. The more you give, the more you will receive. You will never go bankrupt from loving.

In the next chapter we will look at forgiveness, an often-necessary companion to the transforming power of love.

SEVEN

Forgive like a Child

Forget to Remember,
Remember to Forget

A church in Ohio was having such major relational problems that District Superintendent Arthur Parsons had to be called in as a negotiator. After the group had sung the old hymn "Blest Be the Tie that Binds," but just before the business session was to begin, Art spotted a little boy sitting in the front row. He had big brown eyes and was smiling peacefully.

Art found out the little guy's name, brought him up beside the podium and put an arm around his shoulder.

"Joey," Art asked, "do you hate anyone?"

Joey grinned. "No."

"Joey, do you love everybody?"

Joey's reply was immediate. "Yes!"

"And Jesus called a little child to Him, [and] set him in the midst of them" (Matthew 18:2). Art Parsons knew that the solution to most friction is in becoming like children in our forgiving and forgetting.

Charles Swindoll uses an illustration in one of his books that points to the tremendous danger of unforgiveness. He tells about a woman who was found dead. Beside her body was a suicide note that started, "They said. . . ." She never completed telling what "they said," but whatever it was, it was painful enough to seem reason for extinguishing her own life.

I cannot get away from the spiritual and practical application of those nursery rhymes that speak volumes to children. This one, from *Old Mother Goose and Other Nursery Rhymes*, applies to the above situation:

> There were once two cats of Kilkenny,
> Each thought there was one cat too many;
> So they fought and they fit,
> And they scratched and they bit,
> Till, excepting their nails
> And the tips of their tails,
> Instead of two cats, there weren't any.

Unforgiveness produces two losers. In understanding be adults, but in malice be children. They may fight frequently, but they have the best "forgetters" in the world when it comes to holding grudges.

I have observed an interesting paradox about children. They forget to remember . . . and remember to forget.

Forget to Remember

Yes, children forget to remember. They can be engaged in a hot skirmish, quarreling loudly, and before you can get out the door to referee the fight, they have called a truce and are sharing their M & Ms with the enemy.

No wonder Jesus emphasized repeatedly, "And a little child shall lead them." After you have given a child something, or showed him or her a kindness, he or she forgets that earlier you withheld an item or a privilege. A child forgets to remember.

To their mothers' displeasure, children even forget to remember time. If your mental computer is on overload, be like a child: Indulge in something so relaxing and pleasant that you lose track of time. This is why I walk the beach, ride my bike and sing in the choir at church. There are times when I am under such deadline pressure that I wish I could throw away my clock, burn my calendar and have my telephone and doorbell disconnected. Children are not prisoners of these handicaps! They forget to remember.

As adults we must learn this valuable principle. After all, you cannot unspill anything. You cannot saw sawdust. That was then and this is now.

One psychiatrist used a rather crude illustration when he said, "Picking your nose when you are alone is still picking your nose." Translation: Harboring grudges and revenge, whether you display them publicly and rehearse your resentment or hold them in, is still sin. Relishing your hate toward the person who wronged you is sin. Someone once said, "He who refuses to forgive breaks the bridge over which he himself must pass to get to God." Even if someone does not deserve your forgiveness, offer it. If you regard iniquity in your heart, God is deaf. He will not, cannot hear your prayers when you hang onto unforgiveness, even if the person by whom you have been hurt was totally in the wrong. (See Mark 11:26, Luke 6:37.)

The Word tells us, "Blessed are the peacemakers" (Matthew 5:9). Not the pacemaker—the peacemaker. Being right is not nearly as important as being the peacemaker.

A young husband at a couples' retreat asked us confidentially to pray for his marriage.

"I wish Janelle didn't have such a good memory," he said. "I appreciate the fact that she is so punctual about paying the bills, balancing the checkbook and managing the house efficiently. But when we were first married she was raking leaves one day and yelled out as I left for work, 'Bring home a wheelbarrow.' I suggested that she use a box, since we had just bought this little house in the country and were totally broke. I explained that the leaf season was about over and next year we could afford some yard equipment. She yelled, 'Scrooge!' at me as I left the driveway. Since then I have bought her a new Buick LeSabre, and we have had eight exciting and loving years of marriage. But anytime she wants to hurt me she brings up the wheelbarrow incident and calls me 'Scrooge.'"

My husband counsels many professional men who leave nit-picking, nervous, quarreling women who make too many demands, to run off with "airheads" who are easier to please and able to laugh. We have also observed, while listening to husbands guilty of infidelity, that over and over again they almost all say the same thing: "I hated myself the first time I did this. I did not have a good time because I had this awful guilt hanging over my head. I would have returned home the very next morning, penitent, but I knew I would hear her bring it up over and over again, trying to even the score."

A word for brides: There are a lot of bums out there, and a great shortage of good men. If you do not want your husband, put him on the back porch when you go to bed tonight. There will be nine women standing in line to get him by morning.

For every woman who makes a fool of a man, there is a creative woman standing by who can make a man of a fool. Which kind are you? In marriage, it is often good to forget to remember.

There are two things I never wanted to be when I grew up: a stepmother and a mother-in-law. Nearly every fairy tale has an evil, hideous, vicious, unfair stepmother, and some of the funniest—but often most unkind and resent-ful—jokes are poked at mothers-in-law. But when I said, "I do" to Carl, I became both a stepmother and a mother-in-law instantly. Now I have understanding and empathy for each of those states in life.

At one women's retreat I did a session on depression and weight control. I gave each young woman a three-by-five card and asked her to write out her deepest personal need, without signing her name. I promised that our front-line warriors back home in Clearwater would be praying.

One woman's request really spoke to this issue of unforgiveness and got through to me. It read: "Pray for my mother-in-law. She cuts me down till I feel I am only three feet tall. She can't seem to remember the eighteen years of happiness and three children I have given her son, but she can't seem to *forget* the clumsy adjustment she and I made when I was a new, eighteen-year-old, nervous and anxious bride."

Can't seem to remember, can't seem to forget. That is the essence of unforgiveness.

But you can break its cycle by forgetting to remember. Invest in this wonderful adventure of forgiveness. It yields great rewards of interest. When you are angry and unforgiving, you allow resentment to live in your head without paying rent. You will probably not hurt the person you are resenting, but will instead make yourself sick. Do your homework to avoid depression, ulcers and sleeplessness: Empty your mental computer of resentment. No one else can do it for you. Forget to remember.

Remember to Forget

Scotch-taped to the front of our refrigerator is a three-word gem: "Get over it." If I had the money, I would buy a thousand T-shirts and have this printed in large, bold letters on the front. I would give one to several people I know, and many I do not know yet.

Remember to forget. Do it deliberately for your own good health and mental well-being.

I played the organ one afternoon recently at the funeral service for a man I will call Burton. He was only 57 when he died, and had not seemed to be ill. Our families go to the same doctor, so I asked him, "What caused Burton's death?"

"He died a year ago," the doctor replied. "We only buried him today. He wasn't sick. He died of a broken heart; his wife and two sons killed him."

The doctor went on to tell me that Burton's first wife had died, and he had remarried. While the two grown sons and their families were vacationing together during the summer, the older son dug up something from their father's past, dwelt upon and enlarged it, thus betraying his dad. This caused the younger son to reject his father. The venom of the experience had been "under the blood" for 31 years, but when the new wife learned about it, she allowed herself to be affected to the point that she developed a self-righteous attitude of disrespect and dishonor, which turned to disdain and hate. Even though Burton tried to explain the situation and never quit loving his wife and sons, they never regained their respect for him. His hurt heart burst, and he just quit living.

If you want your family tree traced, get into the ministry or politics. One experience of the past can be inflated by the media and eradicate from the minds of thinking people a lifetime of good behavior, benevolence and charity. In journalism we call it the "poison pen." But we Christians have no business using the poison pen. If God has forgiven, we should at least try to forget.

The book of Proverbs tells us that three things cannot be recalled: youth, a shot arrow once it leaves the bow and words that have already been spoken. As a child I saw a vivid parable that illustrates the truth of that verse.

My grandmother, Mom Burns, had four prize bed pillows. They were made of blue and white pin-striped ticking, plumply filled with goosedown feathers. One day when I was very small I helped her plump them up and hang them on the clothesline to air in the sunshine.

During lunch we looked out the window and thought it was snowing—but it was early June! One of the pillowcases had broken open and feathers were flying in every direction. We rushed out with a box and picked up a large pile that had fallen directly under the clothesline, but there was no way we could recall the thousands of soft, tiny, feathers that were blown away. A year later when we picked tomatoes and cucumbers from the garden, we found white feathers attached to the vegetables. We found them in the creek, too, and in birds' nests and stuck to windowpanes on rainy days.

Watch your words; like Mom Burns' feathers, they can never be recalled. The power of life and death are in the tongue, says Proverbs 18:21. Speaking words that wound is an invisible crime, and people who engage in this hurtful activity usually reap a "full-circle" harvest: The hurt comes back, as the old adage puts it, like "chickens come home to roost."

People lose their physical lives because of little things. A ball in the street or a new bicycle received on Christmas can cause a careless accident, and a life is gone.

Likewise, people's emotional and spiritual lives suffer because of small issues. A wife's day is ruined because in a rush, late for work, her husband forgot to kiss her goodbye. The largest misunderstandings and fatal misfortunes usually stem from the smallest issues, soon forgotten, but the penalties linger on.

When we lived in New Castle, Indiana, we watched a business partnership and friendship between two families disintegrate over a small, on-the-job misunderstanding about the cement footing for a foundation! One partner, Mr. Underwood, said the footing needed to be twenty inches deep. Later the other partner, Mr. Frost, said Mr. Underwood embarrassed him publicly by telling the foreman that he had said 22 inches!

"I'm from Kentucky," Mr. Underwood told my husband, "and you don't get a second chance to make a Kentuckian mad. I will never forgive him."

When bids were opened for the next building project, Mr. Underwood decided to spite Mr. Frost: He just did not show up. His stubbornness cost him the business partnership. He was even angrier when Mr. Frost seemed to prosper more than ever before.

Mr. Underwood was just as stubborn on another point. He refused to give his wife the satisfaction of going to church with her. "Only sissies and women go to church," he insisted.

Only two weeks before he choked to death with emphysema, Mr. Underwood admitted he needed God, believed on Jesus Christ and humbled himself to pray, "Lord, I need You. Be merciful to me, a sinner. I want and need eternal life." His little wife danced around their home, thanking God and saying, "Dad, I've waited 62 years to hear you say that."

Yes, Mr. Underwood's story had a happy ending. But what a shame to live on unforgiveness and stubbornness for so many years of a short life! And why couldn't he have given his wife the satisfaction of being a lifetime partner for a purpose, praying and reading the Bible with her and watching Christian television, as he did the last two weeks he was on earth?

Part of the definition of *maturity* is to suffer small hurts without complaining, to be misunderstood without explaining. Jesus told Peter, "What is that to you? You follow me!" (John 21:22). In other words, don't sweat the small stuff. God cannot remember what I cannot seem to forget.

Far too many church troubles are caused by insignificant issues that become big because of a small person's pride. But we are in a spiritual war, folks, and there is no room for sissies in this war, no bargain basement, no cheap Jesus. We need to build ourselves up in the most holy faith (see Jude 20) and refuse to waste cannon balls on mosquitoes.

Ignore petty differences. What will they matter five years from now? Will they affect the Kingdom to come? Bury anything that will prevent you from putting Jesus first. A big person—a Holy-Spirit-filled person—can afford to be magnanimous. Get over it. Remember to forget.

Start Anytime

Our church's Pastor Lambert has a bit of Alabama lingo that I like. He says, "More than once in my life, I kicked the ball when I should have caught it, but I pulled up my jaw from between my knees and started over."

We can do that with forgiveness: We can realize we have been remembering things we should forget, and determine to change our pattern.

My neighbor Dollie lives in the little pink house just east of me. She lived a nightmare of a life for many years and told me once, "I have been so angry and disappointed with life, I wanted to put my head in the oven." (In her childhood home there was always a gas oven, and putting your head in it with the gas jets on full force was considered the quickest and most painless way to commit suicide.) I have, in fact, seen Dollie so angry with others that she would suggest loudly, "Why don't you put your head in the oven?"

Finally Dollie realized that, like a child, she needed a father, a heavenly Father—God. She began her new life with a new pattern: a pattern of forgetting to remember.

That is God's way. The Bible tells us that Jesus came not to condemn the world, or hold it in unforgiveness, but so that we might be saved and reconciled with God (see John 3:17). Jesus told the story of the good shepherd who left 99 sheep inside the fold so he could go out to find the one who

had strayed. Jesus, our Good Shepherd, does not count the
sheep to brag about how many there are in His flock; He
counts them to see who is missing. His rod is for counting,
not for beating, and His staff is for lifting and correction.
"Your rod and Your staff, they comfort me" (Psalm 23:4).
What comfort His forgiveness brings when I have strayed
and deserve His anger!

Since Jesus set us this example of forgiveness, we sheep
need to comfort each other, too. We must not fight, but forgive. We must not talk against and about each other, but
against and about our mutual enemy, Satan.

Once again the book of Proverbs says it best:

> Hatred stirs up strife,
> But love covers all sins.
> 10:12

> Pleasant words are like a honeycomb,
> Sweetness to the soul and health to the bones.
> 16:24

> A whisperer separates the best of friends.
> 16:28

> He who covers a transgression seeks love,
> But he who repeats a matter separates the best of friends.
> 17: 9

We need to cover for each other. I do not mean we should
lie, but that we should let our love cover another's faults
until he gets his act together. Charity, says 1 Peter 4:8, covers a multitude of sins.

Our friends Jeff and Bonnie Rueb wrote some time ago
to tell Carl and me about an experience that has cemented
forever their understanding of forgiveness. I want to share
their story in their words:

When our son T.J. was born, the doctor reported, "You've got a football player here!" And football was always T.J.'s dream. He grew to be a big kid, 5 feet 11 inches and 210 pounds at the age of fifteen.

We didn't fret too much when the school called one day to tell us that T.J. had suffered an injury and would be hospitalized. The police and principal had T.J. write out a statement. This was unreal, a nightmare. He was clowning around with friends on the way to class and another student took offense at the boys' lighthearted conversation. He followed our son into the classroom, grabbed a T-square from the drafting table and cleaved a one-inch gash deep into our son's head while his friends watched, near hysterics.

This couldn't be happening to us. We were law-abiding citizens with good kids, pastors of a local church. We didn't know how to entertain terms like *felony assault*, *press charges*, or *juvenile probation department*.

After a CAT scan the neurosurgeon, Dr. Mark Kubala, explained that the blow came very near to severing the cerebral artery. It could have caused death or permanent damage to the area of the brain that controls motor skills. We didn't even have medical insurance. We prayed; what else could we do?

The necessary craniotomy required two hours and was successful. T.J.'s progress was remarkable, and he needed not even so much as Tylenol for pain following the surgery. He was alert and hungry.

When T.J. was released we learned that he would have to finish his freshman year at home with a tutor, and never play football again. We were also faced with $14,000 in medical bills and no way to pay them. Should we file a lawsuit? What would happen to T.J.'s attacker?

The next year was a blur of paperwork, phone calls, doctors' visits, consultations with attorneys, dealing with anger and frustration and praying for God's help through it all. As the months passed, God brought forgiveness and healing to all of us. We in turn forgave the violator who perpetrated the assault and we prayed for his salvation. God turned the hearts of the juvenile probation officers, attorneys, insurance companies, hospitals, doctors and even the Attorney General's office of the State of Texas in our favor. The medical bills were paid! In addition, a small sum was set aside in a trust fund that will be available when T.J. turns eighteen.

The scar on T.J.'s head is a daily reminder that he is a second-chance person. The investment of childlike forgiveness healed the situation and moved the hand of God. He turned around what the enemy meant for evil and made it "work together for good" (Romans 8:28) because we had loved the Lord and forgiven the enemy. It was our redemption also.

In his second letter to the Corinthians, Paul wrote,

We're not in charge of how you live out the faith, looking over your shoulders, suspiciously critical. We're partners, working alongside you, joyfully expectant. I know that you stand by your own faith, not by ours. . . . I don't want to come down too hard [on the person who caused all this pain] . . . Now is the time to forgive this man and help him back on his feet. If all you do is pour on the guilt, you could very well drown him in it. My counsel now is to pour on the love.

1:24; 2:5–8, TM

Jeff and Bonnie Rueb chose to forgive the transgressor and pour their love on him in their actions and attitudes. They triumphed in Christ and spread His fragrance all around, by forgetting to remember and remembering to forget. You, too, can start anytime to pattern your memory in the likeness of a child, for Jesus' sake.

In chapter 8 we will look at the last factor in childlikeness. I call it "relying and relaxing."

EiGHT

Rely and Relax like a Child

God Is Still in Charge

t was forty minutes before flight time. I was traveling between Tampa and St. Louis, and the line at the ticket counter seemed endless. Grown-ups were prancing, chewing gum much too fast and looking at wristwatches they had already looked at four times in less than a minute. Finally it was my turn to talk to the ticket agent.

That was when I saw them standing directly behind me: a young mother and her little son. He was sleeping soundly, peacefully, in this line of tense adults, draped across her shoulder, completely unaware of her actions in buying their tickets. The little fellow never did know when we boarded; he was still relaxed in sleep, totally relying on his mother. She must have been reliable: He simply trusted her to be in charge, to take care of all the arrangements.

As I settled finally into my seat on the plane, I thought of the words of the old hymn, "Oh, what peace we often forfeit, oh, what needless pain we bear." The Bible speaks often of the fact that we can trust our heavenly Father to be in charge, to care for our "arrangements":

> Under the shadow of His wings you can trust (rely). (See Psalm 17:8; 36:7; 91:1.)
> Jesus would have gathered Jerusalem under His wings as a mother hen shields her chicks. (See Matthew 23:37.)
> The Lord will perfect that which concerns me. (See Psalm 138:8.)

But do we believe He is in charge? Do we take Him at His Word? Do we trust, rely, relax under His protection? All too often the answer is no.

Children are survivors because they know how to rely on God (or His surrogates in their lives, their parents) and relax. They are pioneers, leaders in this field. They seem to be born with the instinct to rely, and are specialists at relaxing. This is another essential we can learn from them. Once again, "A little child shall lead them." Let's consider what it means to rely on God and to relax in His arms.

Relying on God

Rely is only a four-letter word, but putting it into action offers us a wealth of confidence as we depend on God. A child almost always believes her father, even if he is an airhead or a windbag. Our heavenly Father is neither, and He is utterly reliable. His Word is truth. We can trust Him.

When I talk about relying as children do, I do not mean to suggest that we should be overbearing, overly familiar or presumptuous with God. I once met a bold young woman who showed me her driver's license. It read, "Connie, Jesus' Daughter." That was it; she refused to use her given name. To me she seemed to be thumbing her nose at man's laws.

Jesus said we were to "render unto Caesar the things that are Caesar's," not to flaunt our freedom in Jesus in the face of those who may not know Him. That is not relying on God; that is a form of cocky self-confidence.

I learned one of my greatest lessons in true reliance from my daughter Brenda. When I was 28 years old and Brenda was six, she slipped off a fishing pier along the Wabash River. I tried to rescue her and almost drowned both of us. A man standing by helped us out of the water.

To my amazement, Brenda did not seem to be frightened by the experience, but came up coughing and saying matter-of-factly, "I've got to learn how to swim!" Why wasn't she afraid? She knew I was in charge; she knew I was there to take care of her.

I love this line from the old song Ethel Waters used to sing: "When the storms of life are raging, stand by me." God's Word promises that God will be there to take care of us, too. He will stand by us. But the prophet Isaiah tells us we have a part to play when those storms are raging. He says, "In returning and rest you shall be saved; in quietness and confidence shall be your strength" (30:15). In other words, rely.

When I was growing up, my dad was also my pastor. Even after sitting for all those years in church, I remember only a few of his sermons. I usually spent that time in the service unwrapping Kraft's caramels as quietly as possible and sharing them with my two little friends, Rose Alice Beatty and Margaret Nagy.

But one message I have never forgotten. Dad read from John 14:27: "Let not your heart be troubled, neither let it be afraid." Then he continued, "When the boat is in the water, that's good. But when the water gets into the boat, that's bad. In this world you will have trouble, but don't let the trouble ever enter your heart. If you commit your work to the Lord, your plans will be established" (see Proverbs

16:3). Dad went on, "With God you never lose; you just practice until you win."

That is bedrock to rely on! But human as we are, we keep forgetting that we can trust His timing and His ways.

One day a few years ago I jumped into my old MGA and headed for the beach. I had just positioned my pelican beach towel and was lying lazily, listening to the chatter of the seagulls, when suddenly I felt dizzy, too hot and very sick. The sun never makes me sick; usually I can stay on the beach for hours. Frustrated, I obeyed the nudge of my body to hurry home.

When I arrived, a message was coming through on our answering machine. April Dawn was in the Mease Hospital emergency room. She had been involved in an accident on a jet ski, and her leg had been deeply split.

"Why, Lord?" April asked. So did we. She was working in Gainesville, Florida, and needed the money. The accident caused her to lose eleven days of work.

But during the time April was recuperating in the hospital and then at home, the Gainesville college campus killings took place. As you undoubtedly remember, a man committed gory murders of several young women who lived alone. April had been living only two blocks from the scene of these crimes.

"Why, Lord?" we had asked. *Trust Me, My children.* The accident was a blessing in disguise. Oh, how we need to rely on Him.

Relaxing in God's Arms

Earlier I mentioned our friends Paul and Tracy Hamelink, who currently pastor a church in Green Bay, Wisconsin. One autumn Sunday when I spoke there, the congregation had planned a book autograph party in the church foyer between Sunday school and the morning worship service.

Time was limited, so we were moving fast. Some folks set up a table and a large number of people were scurrying around: Ushers were rushing, greeters were hugging, pastors were shaking hands, musicians were arriving with instruments and I was talking and autographing books as quickly as I could. There was standing room only.

At one point I overheard a concerned young father who was standing in line ask his wife, "Where's Mitch?" I looked up to see an usher grin and point. In the midst of the traffic, young Mitch, a trusting two-year-old, had stretched out on the floor and fallen asleep. Large feet were tramping all around him and the foyer was noisy, but Mitch was a free spirit, totally confident and trusting that no harm would come to him, sleeping with a "ho-hum" smile on his wee face. Mitch knew how to rely and relax.

So did another little boy named Bobby. He was born with osteogenesis imperfecta congenita (OI), which is nicknamed "brittle bone disease." Most babies with Bobby's degree of OI die at birth, but Bobby's parents provided an atmosphere of Christian love in which he thrived emotionally and spiritually for sixteen and a half years.

Once when Bobby was hospitalized, he told his family, "I was in heaven with Jesus. He and I looked down on the world and the devil. Mom, I'm not scared; the devil ain't nothing!" Bobby's absence of fear in the presence of God enabled him to relax in the Father's arms during his brief life.

Our friend Elmer Church wrote this poem about Bobby's impact on his life:

I saw God's holy light
While shopping in a store one day.
A woman chanced to pass my way,
In her arms a baby boy, her only child, her pride and joy.

Although four years old, about eight months in size,
Beautiful, beautiful and so wise.
Born to stir hearts, his worth more than gold.
Born with a bone disease, his pain was untold.

From out of his tiny baby's fleshly cloak,
'Twas the voice of God that spoke.
Hidden in the depths of his eyes so bright
I caught a glimpse of God's holy light.

Our God has jewels upon this earth,
And gems such as this need no new birth.
Someday with angels in heaven he'll be,
In a glorified body, from pain set free.

This tiny boy made my heart rejoice,
Oh, truly, truly, I heard God's voice.
All you need do is look at this child,
To see how God's face looks, when Bobby smiled.

When Bobby died he had never walked, and he was only as tall as a three-year-old. But he left with us a message, an example of a life relaxed in God's arms.

My husband has a motto: "Anything worth doing is worth doing fast." My motto, on the other hand, is: "Anything worth doing is worth sipping, and out of doors."

But I have not always been so relaxed. After Brenda's near-disaster on the Wabash, I realized that at 28 years of age I loved the water, but I did not understand it. So I called the Y.W.C.A. and enrolled Brenda and myself in a swimming class.

I fretted all morning before the first lesson. *What will all those little kids think of a woman of 28, sticking out like a sore thumb in a class of thirty children?* I asked myself. To my surprise I was not the only adult in the group. A grandmother who had watched a small child she was baby-sitting drown in a pool was also there to learn.

"I am haunted by the fact and can't sleep at night," she told me, "knowing that I could have saved little Melinda if I had only known how to swim."

The thirty children learned quickly to relax. But the instructor had a hard time convincing the old lady and me that we could float and would not drown if we would lie on our backs, look up at the ceiling, breathe slowly through our mouths and relax. She pleaded with us, "Rely on me! I get paid for this; I do it a hundred times each day."

Finally I did it: I relaxed, I relied on the instructor and I can not only float, I can swim!

If you really want to relax, invite Jesus into your life. Then cultivate one human friend you can relax with, someone who is totally childlike and uncomplicated in the way Jesus is. I have one friend who is so uncoordinated that she cannot walk and chew gum at the same time, but she is my cheerleader, easy to be with. She cannot pronounce a lot of words, so she does not check my spelling and punctuation; nor does she expect me to qualify every statement I make. I have, I need, I respect editors; my books would not be digestible without them. But I need a friend I can be a kid with, one who does not care how I look, dress or act.

I have friends who must have a direct fax line from God. They know when I am down. A friend from Phoenix sent a simple note one day that read, "May His hand rest softly on your heart." She had no idea that I had just had my heart lacerated by a harsh judgment and false accusation.

Before I met Carl I almost married a man because his expectations were so simple. I asked him, "What are you looking for in a mate?"

"I have only one qualification," he replied quickly. "I want someone to relax with."

Relax in the love of Jesus and build a friendship with someone who knows how to do the same.

Keys to Survival

As I have watched children rely and relax, I have observed five keys to their simple, sturdy survival. We can learn a great deal about unlocking the doors of reliance and relaxation if we study these keys.

Key #1: Prayer

When I was a little girl, I heard the accomplished Myron Floren play his accordion on the radio. (Years later he showed up on "The Lawrence Welk Show.") I was entranced, and for Christmas that year I asked my parents for an accordion.

I should have known it could not happen. We were poorer than poor. But children don't know it cannot happen; they just rely. After I talked to my parents, I talked to God one night. "Lord," I prayed, "if You get me an accordion for Christmas, I will play at church, at nursing homes and at jail services, and I will never play songs with bad words."

One day shortly before Christmas, while playing hide-and-seek with my brothers, I hid in Mom and Dad Burns' old farmhouse attic. I actually was not surprised to find an accordion also hiding there, waiting for Santa to deliver it on Christmas Eve. Several times when I was alone in the house, I took the delightful opportunity to get it out, touch it, practice with it. My parents thought it miraculous that on Christmas morning, when we woke up and opened our gifts, I was a natural with that accordion!

A child's confidence in prayer is worth learning. I had a winning combination: my Dad and my God. (Are you part of a winning combination for your children or grandchildren?)

Remember, you are merely the pray-er. God is the prayer answer-er. Mature praying consists of total dependence on

God and responsible action on the part of the one who prays.

Reminisce magazine recently stimulated my thinking on the difference between reliance and luck. "Many people pray but rely on gambling and good luck charms," I read. "Take the rabbit's foot, for instance. It sure didn't help the rabbit!"

Prayer is not mumbling into your mattress at bedtime; it is not worrying out loud. Prayer is talking to God, making known your needs and some of your wants, then relying and relaxing. Some theological genius once said, "If you are going to pray, don't worry; if you are going to worry, don't pray."

I believe the key to getting our prayers answered is to pray the promises. Praying the Word clears away religious confusion and uncertainty. You can pray powerfully and in the will of God. Then you can freely receive everything that the Word has promised.

Key # 2: Receiving and Obeying Instructions

When Charlton Heston trained to drive a chariot in one of the epic Bible movies for which he became famous, he had trouble staying on the rapidly moving contraption.

"I am supposed to win this chariot race," he told his director, William Wyler, "and I can barely stay on this thing."

"Your job is to stay on the chariot," Wyler answered. "It's my job to make sure you win."

If Hollywood can work "miracles" and even arrange for winners, why do we fail to trust in the power of the almighty God of the universe? Our job is to get our instructions from Him (through prayer and the reading and hearing of His Word) and then to obey them.

I was doing an autograph party at a bookstore in Greenville, South Carolina, when a lady stopped by with her little boy. She wanted a book very much, but looking into her purse realized that she had no money.

Then her little boy spoke up. "Mommy," he said with the serene confidence of a child, "you don't ever need money if you have your Visa card."

If only we could have that kind of confidence in the Word of God and in God's ability to supply our needs! Children take Bible verses literally and personally. Lois Mitchell's little granddaughter quoted from the 23rd Psalm: "Surely goodness and mercy shall follow me all the days of my life." She stopped to think.

"Is that true, Grandmama?" she asked. "I don't like Shirley, and I don't want her following me!"

When little children receive instructions, they rely on them. In their relationships with God, they pray, then relax in the fact that God has heard.

We have a book of instructions, the Bible, and an Instructor we can trust. He is the God who inspired the writing of the instructions. Second Corinthians 4:8–9 offers a childlike approach:

We are hard pressed on every side, yet not crushed; we are perplexed, but not in despair; persecuted, but not forsaken.

The Christian life is not the subtraction of trials, but the addition of power to overcome them. We can be sick in victory or well in victory. Jesus fought the battle, but the victory is ours; we simply have to obey His instructions, holding fast without wavering, as a baby holds onto his mother's breast until he is fully nourished and totally satisfied. God honors that kind of obedience.

To be led by the Holy Spirit does not mean to shift your brain into neutral, but to put your soul under His control, thus shifting your engine into overdrive to take the strain off your motor. It takes the guesswork out of living and the fear out of dying.

After your first simple, initial prayer, "Lord, be merciful to me, a sinner," God hears every prayer you pray. (This is because you have been born of the Spirit.) Walking in the Spirit, living in the Spirit and being led by the Spirit simply involve obeying the Instructor and the instructions. God will never tell you to do something that goes against the authority of His Book. And He always knows what He is doing, even when we do not think so. As 1 Corinthians tells us,

> The foolishness of God is wiser than men, and the weakness of God is stronger than men. . . . Not many wise according to the flesh, not many mighty, not many noble, are called. But God has chosen the foolish things of the world to put to shame the wise, and God has chosen the weak things of the world to put to shame the things which are mighty; and the base things of the world and the things which are despised God has chosen, and the things which are not, to bring to nothing the things that are. . . . Of Him you are in Christ Jesus, who became for us wisdom from God—and righteousness and sanctification and redemption—that, as it is written, "He who glories, let him glory in the Lord."
>
> 1 Corinthians 1:25–31

That is why we can receive His instructions with child-like trust and obey them.

"Any fool can prove the Bible ain't so," quipped Josh Billings. "But it takes a wise man to believe it."

A wise man—as wise as a child.

Key #3: Contentment

I had started to turn off the lamp beside my hotel room bed so I could go to sleep when I spotted an official visitors' guide. The front cover read, "Table of Content." Although I was almost asleep, a clever graphic artist had commanded my attention with an ad for a steak house! Tables in that restaurant were considered to be "tables of content." Hmmm. "Relax, have fun, rely on our expert chefs to select the finest cuts of USDA choice beef for your steak," said the ad.

It is strange how Scriptures memorized when you were a small child will surface at such times. "You prepare a table before me" (Psalm 23:5) and "Godliness with contentment is great gain" (1 Timothy 6:6) popped into my mind. Contentment with a steak dinner seemed pretty chintzy compared to the contentment and satisfaction God offers.

Before the days of automatic dishwashers, Mom Perky, my paternal grandmother, was helping me with the dishes after dinner. I complained a smidgen about the cramped quarters of our two-room upstairs apartment. She shook her head and said, "Bets, the happiest women I know live in tents." Then she went on to quote that verse from 1 Timothy: "Godliness with con*tent*ment is great gain."

Contentment is another lesson we can learn from children. I have about everything Erma Bombeck has ever written. I thrive on her banter and word play. The public has learned that she has battled cancer. She receives great satisfaction, she says, while volunteering in a hospital ward for children with cancer. For one frail little girl who might not live until Christmas, Erma decided to have Christmas a little early. "What would you like?" she asked the child.

Her sweet reply: "Erma, I have two sticker fun books and a Cabbage Patch doll. I already have everything."

That little girl's contentment made me ashamed and broke my mother's heart.

To be content with such things as we have, says the writer of Hebrews, is an admirable state for a Christian (13:5). Yet we are not content with our wages, our ages, our location, our mate, our hair color, our car or who we are.

One of my neighbors was sitting at her dressing table preparing for bedtime while her little grandson, Tony, looked on.

"Grandma, what's that stuff you took out of the refrigerator to put under your eyes?" She informed him that every night she applied cooled, age-defying (denying?) cream to get rid of the lines around her eyes. Turning his little head sideways he commented, "It's not working, is it?"

Simplicity. Contentment. Have you ever realized how vain we are? I spoke at a women's conference held in a monastery in Madison, Wisconsin. We stayed in the nuns' rooms, each of which contained a simple desk, asphalt tile floors, a small bed, a very small closet and no mirrors. Do you realize how much time we spend looking into those looking glasses? Fretting in the mirror will not make you any taller, nor shorten your gawky height. Relax; don't be so preoccupied with getting that you cannot respond to God's giving. Look at the lilies and wildflowers. They bloom even if people do not go to the country or walk in the meadows to see them. He will see to your needs, too. (See Matthew 6:28.)

My singer friend Lillie Knauls paraphrases Paul's words to express her philosophy of contentment: "My God promised to supply all my needs, so if I don't have it, I don't need it." (See Philippians 4:19.)

How little we really do need! Leigh Noakes lives in Safety Harbor with her parents. Following a terrible wreck that left her with serious brain damage and a lot of paralysis, Leigh is thankful for every step of progress. One Easter she sent me a pretty card with a note that read, "I am sleeping upstairs now, and so happy that I suddenly am able to climb stairs. Now I must lose weight." How Leigh's simple contentment touched me. And I complain because I live in a stilt house that requires me to climb sixteen steps!

When Carl and I first married, he had just returned from India where he was a missionary for several years. He had never seen a "Toys R' Us" store, and he wept when we walked into the one here in Clearwater.

"Why are you crying?" I asked.

"There are more toys in this one store than in all the country of India," he answered. "The children kick cans, whittle wood to create toys and work in the gardens for recreation. Several children in one family ride the same bike." Carl told me how amazing he thought it that the little ones survived even when they were hungry, because they were loved, and were content with love. Every street was filled with adults carrying small children on their hips. They loved their children, and their children survived, simply.

When our son, Carl David, his wife, Diane, and my husband returned from a trip down memory lane to the India of their earlier lives, they sent a video to Carl's daughter, Carol, who had lived there also. Her response was profound. Here is a portion of her letter:

> We have just spent two days in court, prompted by [the complaints of] two disgruntled ladies who didn't want us to have an office in our home, though the law clearly allows it. The judge was totally disinterested. Jack [her husband] and I came home weary from the ridiculous ordeal to find the video you sent from India. What a contrast! The letters and pictures brought back memories of the simple childhood there, when life seemed so worry-free and carefree. The children still seem so unaffected, unspoiled, untarnished, and show facial expressions of simple joy and innocence. What a blissful way of life!

Yet a blissful way of life does not depend on our location, or on how little—or how much—we own. True contentment is a state of mind brought about by our dependence on God.

David Wilkerson tells of crying out, exhausted, mentally drained with compassion fatigue, complaining to God. Then, like a kid, he suddenly realized the promises God has made through His Word. David began to see himself as rich—rich in strength, writing a check and drawing on the promises deposited in his account. In God he had everything!

Be content.

Key #4: Babylike Sleep

Have you noticed how readily babies fall asleep in the midst of the busiest of circumstances?

Dunedin, Florida, is the sister city of Sterling, Scotland, and sports bagpipers complete with plaid kilts and a marching band. One day during a parade I watched a darling pair of twins leaning back in their double stroller in deep sleep, oblivious to the parade, the cheering people and the bagpipes whining out their joyous strains of music.

A similar scene was enacted in Tissy's Boutique one mid-afternoon. A two-year-old tot had been following his mother back and forth from the dress rack to the dressing room. Suddenly I missed him. Where was he? Curled up in the line of traffic in front of the checkout counter, relaxed and engaged in a deep and satisfying nap.

Babylike sleep. If we could make and sell a pill that would guarantee it, we would become both rich and famous. But I believe children, by their example, trust and simplicity, can point us in the direction of a sure 'nough guarantee that is better than any pill. It is the peace promised to us by Jesus.

There is a place in God where we can sleep like babies, finding peace in the midst of stormy circumstances. Use key #2 here if sleep is a problem: God's Word has much to say about sleep. Say these verses over to yourself when insomnia threatens:

> I will both lie down in peace, and sleep; for
> You alone, O LORD, make me dwell in safety.
> > Psalm 4:8

> He gives His beloved sleep.
> > Psalm 127:2

> Your sleep will be sweet.
> > Proverbs 3:24

And the peace of God, which surpasses all understanding,
will guard your hearts and minds through Christ Jesus.

Philippians 4:7

One other tip: My common sense paraphrase of 1 Peter
3:10 says, "If you would love life and see good days, don't
rehearse bad news even if it is true." If at all possible, guard
against talking about negative news or fearful things, especially close to bedtime. This will insure that you and your
family will sleep more peacefully.

Children can relax quickly. If you have trouble sleeping,
try what our doctor friend recommends. Go to bed early.
Find a comfortable position. After a silent prayer to God,
talk to your body.

"Head, let go. Neck, let go. Shoulders, let go. Fingers, let
go." Talk to your body all the way to the toes. Let go. It
works. Adults are programmed for speed, but children do
this without instructions.

Sleep like a baby.

Key #5: Minute Vacations

A letter arrived recently from a woman in Marion, North
Carolina, named Clara Birdsong. I have never met her and
have no idea where Marion, North Carolina, is, but I like
the ring of her name—Birdsong.

I thought of Clara Birdsong the other day when I took little Stephanie Shryer for a ride in my old MGA convertible.
At every stop sign and every red light she would sigh and
exclaim, "Aunt Betty, with the top down we can hear the
birds sing."

Robert Lynd must have been a kindred spirit of Stephanie's. He once said, "In order to see the birds, it is necessary to become part of the silence." I have learned something from Stephanie: I need to take minute vacations as
children do. Now, even when the air conditioning is on in

my car, I roll down the windows when I am delayed at a traffic light and listen for the birdsong, just as she taught me to do. I arrive at work or choir rehearsal refreshed because I have relaxed.

As adults we are often so concerned about entertaining each other while we travel together that we cannot relax. What wise person once said, "Don't say anything if you can't improve on silence"? And here is a nugget I picked up from *Bits and Pieces:* "There are two kinds of people who don't say much: those who are quiet and those who talk a lot."

The turbulence of adult life may make it more difficult to rely and relax, but we must find tranquillity, or snap. Even Jesus withdrew to lonely places and prayed (Luke 5:16). Jesus knew how to take minute vacations.

My friend Debbie Barna reminded me of her "minute vacation" Scripture, Zephaniah 3:17: "The Lord . . . will quiet you in His love."

Yesterday I took my own advice and created a minute vacation. I did what I loved to do as a kid: I walked barefoot in the white sand on Clearwater Beach to the north end of the island and back. I ate a chili dog at Palm Pavilion. I took time to fly a kite and saw children watching in pure fascination. I had been so long at my computer that I had forgotten the looks on faces and the expressions of eyes.

What kind of minute vacation works for you? Program it into your schedule on a regular basis.

As Calm As a Child

Years ago we had a little cabin cruiser named the Betty Lynn. After one warm, sunny day on Catarack Lake, near Rockville, Indiana, we decided to spend the night on the boat. We tied up near the shore between two trees and bedded down in the small cabin with Brenda snugly tucked in on an air mattress between the two of us. Engaging in pillow talk, we planned to fry bacon on the back deck next morning for breakfast. We heard Brenda's prayers, then did our "Good night, sweet dreams," Walton's-Mountain-style, and slept soundly.

Suddenly in the night we heard a gust of wind, lightning, thunder and heavy rain. Then a sweet little voice asked, "Daddy, are you afraid?"

"No, Brenda, I'm not afraid."

"Then I'm not afraid either," she whispered, and quickly fell asleep again. She relied and relaxed.

I thought of a sheet of paper Scotch-taped to the inside closet door in our bedroom. It had 48 squares, each containing the same message: "Relax, God is in charge!"

A retired minister challenged me to develop an article entitled "God's Grip Don't Slip!" "I'd rather be living in Romans 8 than in the Garden of Eden," he wrote. "Remember how Dad Perkins told you that Hebrews 13:5 applies to the next generation: 'I will never leave thee nor forsake thee.' It's the only Scripture in the Bible that can be quoted backward, and it still means the same thing: 'Thee forsake, nor thee leave, never will I'!"

It would make a good article. All things do work together for our good, because God is still in charge.

Dr. Louise Doliveira sent me the following quote:

> Let no one faltering say,
> We be too small and weak a company.
> God has with lesser tools than we
> Worked miracles for all to see.

The whole theme of this book on simplicity cries, "Yes!" God will do it if we relax and rely.

NINE

Pass a Legacy
of Simplicity
to the Next Generation

As we work toward recapturing childlike simplicity in our own lives, we need to realize that we are not doing it only for ourselves. Somehow we must communicate to our children and grandchildren, both biological and spiritual, the importance of simplicity.

But children already understand simplicity, you say. After all, we are the ones who are trying to learn from them!

Yes, children model simplicity for us, but only for a short and precious time. Perhaps it is arbitrary to use age seven, the so-called "age of accountability," as a mile marker, since all children develop differently. One child may stay child-like until he or she is ten, while another has lost a child's perspective by the age of five. Regardless, childlike simplicity and innocence appear, unfortunately, to be wearing off earlier and earlier in our sophisticated society.

Our search for simplicity, then, is doubly vital: Besides recapturing it for our own spiritual, mental, emotional and physical well-being, we need to recapture it so we can turn around and model it for the next generation before they are trapped by the world's demanding complexity.

In order to do that, we need to understand the nuts and bolts involved in passing on a legacy. It does not happen automatically. We must have people willing to do the passing, and they (we) need to grasp just what the legacy is. Let's look, first, at what is involved in the act of passing on a legacy.

Where Are the Mentors?

I like to think of the people doing the passing as mentors. The word *mentor,* used a lot these days in institutional circles, means "a wise and trusted counselor or teacher" *(American Heritage Dictionary).*

Mentoring is a biblical concept. Jesus, of course, through the Person of the Holy Spirit, is our ultimate Mentor. He models the perfection of the Father (Matthew 5:48), the fruit (or characteristics) of the Godhead (Galatians 5:22–23) and all of the spiritual gifts (see Romans 12:6–8, 1 Corinthians 12:7–11 and Ephesians 4:11–12).

John 14:17 refers to the Holy Spirit as the "Spirit of truth." That is an essential quality for a mentor—credibility. Without it, both mentor and learner are wasting their time.

John 14:26 goes on to tell us exactly how the Holy Spirit mentors us:

> The Helper, the Holy Spirit, whom the Father will send in My name, He will *teach* you all things, and bring to your remembrance all things that I said to you.
>
> italics mine

Teaching and reminding are ongoing mentoring tasks, because all of us are becoming; we are all in process.

Our truthful Teacher/Reminder/Mentor also "helps in our weakness" (Romans 8:26) and prays for us (Romans 8:26–27).

Does being a mentor sound like a scary task? It should not, because as Christians we have the Holy Spirit living inside us while He does the mentoring. All we have to do is live out what we are learning from Him.

Paul was not afraid to be a mentor. He said, "Follow me as I follow Christ" (see 1 Corinthians 4:16). When we are following Christ our Mentor, we are not afraid for people to look to us for guidance.

Jesus said, "Let your light so shine before men, that they may see your good works and glorify your Father in heaven" (Matthew 5:16). He did not tell us to make it shine, to force it to shine or to brag about it; He simply said, *"Let it. . . ."* Jesus was exhorting us to be mentors.

Who Can Be a Mentor?

Given the power of the Holy Spirit in a person's life, nothing—not age, marital status, ability or inability to bear children, life stage, wealth or poverty, education or lack of it, physical strength or physical weakness—nothing should deter us from being mentors. Anyone can be a mentor.

It should be obvious to you by now that Jesus wanted us to see children as our mentors in this area of simplicity. In Matthew 18:4 He commends their humility, and we have looked at several other areas of life in which children can mentor us.

I heard the true story of a man who had once been very poor, but was now driving a bright, shiny, brand-new car. One day as he was driving down the street, he was moved with compassion at the sight of a pitiful-looking child sitting flat on the curb. He stopped the car to chat with the little boy, who asked immediately, "Are you rich? Where did you get that big new car?"

Humbled by the child's attention, the man told him, "The honest truth is, I am not rich. I did not buy this car. My brother has a lot of money, and he gave me this car." The child's eyes widened, and the driver thought the little fellow would say, "I wish he would buy me a car," or, "I wish I had a brother like your brother." But the words that came out of the little boy's mouth were, "I wish I could be a brother like that."

Wow! Who was the mentor? The adult or the child?

Karen Siddle grew up in a family of eight children and now finds herself learning from her nieces and nephews. One niece asked her, "Aunt Karen, where is my *holy* Bible? I can't find my *holy* Bible. I want my *holy* Bible." Another told her, "I love my *holy* grandma; I want to be just like my *holy* grandma."

Jesus was right: These little ones are connoisseurs of holiness. They know what is authentic and recognize a fraud.

Children mentor each other as well. My friend Nancy Johnson, a pastor's wife, was trying to explain the concept of the Trinity to a group of young children in a confirmation class. Then Bridgett, a bright eight-year-old, raised her hand.

"I understand the Trinity," she said. "It's like Mom; she's trinity: She's an aunt, a mom and a sister. All three are one person, my mother."

But not all mentors are children. My dad called my mother "Superwoman, Magician and a Wonder!" She was a good looker and a good cooker. She could play baseball with my little brothers, sew our clothes, work in the garden and dress up dainty and lovely for a Sunday of playing the piano and teaching a Sunday school class. She was my mentor. She was my mother. I knew she was revered, and I wanted to be like her.

On my first day at West Terre Haute Elementary School, my teacher, Zora Kern, asked us to stand up, give our names and tell what we wanted to be when we grew up.

"My name is Betty Perkins," I told the class, "and when I grow up I want to be a mother." The children all laughed, but I wanted to be a mother then, and I still enjoy being a mother—and a mentor—more than anything else I have ever done.

(That brings up an interesting thought: Have you ever heard a child say, "When I grow up, I want to be a mentor"?)

Our long-time friend Bruce Schoemann is crusade director for the Lowell Lundstrom Ministry in South Dakota. A few years ago he made several calls to the residence of Ron Auck, noted prayer conference speaker and writer of the book *Pentecostals in Crisis*. On one occasion Mr. Auck's seven-year-old son, Ronnie, answered the phone.

"Hello. You have reached the Auck residence. This is Ronnie speaking."

Bruce needed to speak with Ronnie's dad, but he decided to have some fun and match wits with this proper little child.

"This is the office of the President, George Bush. I understand you have a relative living in your home who is very popular, important and influential. Could you arrange for me to speak with that person, please?"

Without hesitancy little Ronnie yelled, "Mom, the President wants to talk to you!" Bruce was glad to learn that some moms are not "missing in action" but are full-time family engineers who have moral clout as genuine mentors of their children.

Samuel's mother, Hannah, was that kind of mentor (see 1 Samuel 1 and 2), and so was Moses' mother, Jochebed, who planned for Moses' safety and future thoughtfully and explicitly (see Exodus 2).

Oh, how we need more fathers as mentors! Billy Graham once told of a night he spent in the home of his young twelve-year-old friend Allan. Someone phoned to report to Allan's father, a pastor, that a member of his church was dead drunk on the street and portraying a bad witness.

Before the father left to deal with the situation, he told his wife, "Put on the monogrammed sheets and freshen up the guest room. I will bring him home and keep him with us for the night."

Billy listened quietly as young Allan told his dad he did not think this was a good idea, since the man might get sick in the night and ruin those expensive monogrammed sheets.

"When he sobers up and awakens tomorrow morning," Allan's father took time to explain kindly, "that man will be so ashamed of himself that he will need all the love, confidence and support we can give him." What an example, what a mentor Allan's father was in modeling the scriptural admonitions that charity (love) covers a multitude of sins (1 Peter 4:8) and that "God is able to graft them in again" (Romans 11:23). You can be sure Allan never forgot such a graphic and close-to-home illustration, and neither did Billy Graham.

My four grandparents were good mentors. They taught us to pray early each morning, read our Bibles each day and have devotions and pray before retiring. It became apparent to us that daily devotions were a priority for our grandparents, a key to survival. At the age of eight I determined that someday I would write a daily devotional. I did. *Morning Jam Sessions* was released in the fall of 1994 and many families are using it. A good share of the credit goes to grandparents who taught me the importance of spending time with God.

Carl and I have a friend who loves to work with kindergarten children. She had one little tyke in her charge who astonished the playground crowd with his profanity.

"Teacher, it's in my head, it's in my head," he said when she approached him.

"God's Word says that 'even a child is known by his deeds' (Proverbs 20:11)," our friend told him. "All of us have two dogs inside of us. One is black and one is white. The black one is bad and the white one is good. The two will always fight, but the one you feed will live and the one you starve and refuse to feed will die."

Children are becoming what we mentors teach them. That teacher is influencing children to become more like Jesus.

God give us more heroes, more mentors! Be one!

A word of caution is in order here. When we commit ourselves to be mentors, we open ourselves up to the scrutiny of those we mentor.

Children scrutinize and start judging at a very young age. I stayed in the home of a young family while conducting a writers' workshop in Wisconsin. Because of the day's planned activities, the youngest boy, whom I will call Tory, did not want to go to school. His dad, whom I assumed was a Christian, picked up the phone and called the school office.

"This is Tory's father. He's very sick and running a fever. He won't be at school today; we're going to take him to the doctor." Then he hung up the phone, winked at Tory and reached out his hand for a "high five."

I would like to check out Tory's integrity ten years from now. Our children usually become like us, not like we would like them to be. They are born originals, but sadly enough die duplicates. This morning I noted for the first time a small brass plaque near the switch on my tape duplicator: "Clean heads periodically. Dirty heads make poor copies." Do you want your children to be duplicates and carbon copies of you? They will, so watch what you model.

"Repentance and forgiveness [are] not the absence of consequences . . . [but] merely the restoration of a relationship," says Jim Schettler. "Sadly enough, whatsoever a man soweth, that shall he also reap, and sooner or later each man sits down to his own private banquet of consequences."

And even sadder is the fact that unhappy, rebellious children are all too often part of those consequences. I am sorry for children born to men who are mere studs, breeders, not fathers, who care more for their golf scores than for their children's grades. And you and I have each met women who are incubators, not mothers; clothes racks, caring more about their social calendars than about their children's health or virtue.

Sitting on the bleachers at a baseball game, I was shocked to hear a loud-mouthed woman say, "I don't care what my kids do or don't do; I don't care what they're taking, where they go or what time they come in, just so I don't know what they're doing and they don't wake me up when they come in."

What a contrast with the way my mother looked at parenting! Someone once asked her, "What does your husband do?" She told them he was a minister.

"What do you do?" the questioner continued.

"I'm in child development," my mother answered. (Why, I wondered, did she grin when she said it?) "I'm a mother; I have three small children."

Mothers are not just incubators who give you free rent inside their wombs for nine months. A publication from the Family Research Council reports that Abe Lincoln was once asked, "What is the greatest book you've ever read?"

"My mother!" was his succinct reply.

And fathers are not mere studs. Forget the spotted owl; responsible fathers are a far more important endangered species.

You can be sure that our children, our children's children and our neighbors' children are watching us, checking us out, looking for integrity, loyalty, forbearance, diligence, commitment and plain old follow-through. "Keep your heart with all diligence," said the writer of Proverbs, "for out of it spring the issues of life" (4:23).

If you have a child who is rebelling, or not compatible with your family's expectations, think it over. Children often absorb the character of the people they spend the most time with. Companions are like elevators. They can take you up or down. Remember, there are good role models (mentors) and bad ones. What is your child's day like? Is he or she using the words of or acting like his or her babysitter or an undesirable friend? If so, it would be worth making some changes. I was a widow with two small children for six years, and know the difficulties some of you encounter in finding good childcare. Pray about these things, and God will make a way.

Marcia Kendall, founder of Flame Fellowship, has organized a women's movement called "Legacy 2000." It has taken off in five South American countries and is being developed here in the United States. Legacy 2000 calls for women to become mentors and intercessors, setting the pace and contending for the faith that was once delivered unto the early saints, so that before the year 2000 all mankind will have tasted real Christianity; and will be drinking from the fountain of living water, Jesus, by the power of His Holy Spirit; and know that Jesus is coming again in the flesh (see 1 Thessalonians 4:17).

Singer Cheryl Watson shares a chorus with the same heart theme that ends with these words: "Revive us, revive us, that our children may walk with God." Mentoring is worth the effort if it will draw our children to Jesus.

The Legacy of Simplicity

Once we decide to be mentors, we need to understand just what the legacy of childlike simplicity is all about. What exactly do we need to pass on?

For me the legacy is all wrapped up in the word *roots*. The idea of "roots" was publicized, of course, by Alex Haley's book of that name and the resulting mini-series that became part of television lore. People are like plants that are rooted, and as folks in our country grasped that word picture, they began to get excited about genealogies and ancestors, old homesteads, customs and family heirlooms.

I want to take our understanding of "roots" a bit further by looking first at the various kinds of roots that make up the legacy of simplicity our children and grandchildren will need to survive in the future.

1. Family Roots

Family roots are foundational, the roots from which the other kinds usually spring. And it is in the shelter of the family that we can most easily mentor our children and grandchildren regarding the childlike, simple values we have discussed in the previous chapters.

My sister-in-law Bobbie Perkins has taught four- and five-year-olds for seventeen years now. Bobbie has noticed that with each new class of children, each new "crop" of tender plants, she recognizes contrasts because of the difference in their roots.

In plant lingo, there is a difference between annuals and perennials: An annual is a plant that lives and blooms for just one year. Annuals have shallow and temporary root systems.

Perennials, on the other hand, have deep tap root systems, making it possible for them to grow and survive "for many years with new herbaceous growth from a perennating part. [They are] persistent, enduring, continuing without interruption, constant, regularly repeated and renewed, recurrent, and continuous, faithfully reproducing, satisfying all requirements" *(Webster's Collegiate Dictionary)*.

Children, like perennials and tall trees, need strong, long tap roots to draw nourishment from the deep resources of God and nature. Give your children the best roots you can, and God will make up the rest.

Author Tim Kimmel does much of his writing at a large rolltop desk. On top are a set of "roots" pictures. To the far left is a photo of the place where he was born. To the far right is a picture of Graceland Cemetery, where he plans to be buried when he dies. In between these two photos is a picture of his wife and children. It is his daily guide, reminding him where his life began, where it will end and what really matters in between.

"The most influential of all educational factors is the conversation in a child's home," said William Temple. And our friend and Jewish philosopher Jerry Dickman insists, "Family is the most important basic of basics, the core and vital heartbeat of living."

Children need strong, firm roots to offer security and boundaries. They do not always understand that they need these—or why.

A young woman recently accused her mother, my friend, "You are prejudiced against a lot of things, including homosexuals."

My friend replied, "I am prejudiced against evil, the devil, crime and sin."

As Billy Graham once put it, "If the father had gone to the hog pen to make the prodigal comfortable in his filth and sin, he would never have come home." Good roots are strong enough to protect a growing plant, to keep it safe.

Life is short. Nurture your roots. Examine them. Examine your parents' roots. Draw nutrition from the roots of their experiments with parenting and with life. And "if it works, don't fix it." There is nothing wrong with tradition if it is good tradition.

A fifteen-year-old once asked a clothing salesman, "If my parents like this suit, may I return it?"

Don't thumb your nose at your parents just to be unique. If you have good roots, don't pull them up. Thomas Edison invented the light bulb a long time ago, but I bought a package of six just this morning, and his concept still sheds light!

So go back to your family roots. Get out some old photos and make some new family memories. The Bible says that in the last days, people will be without natural affection and children will be ungrateful (see Romans 1:31; 2 Timothy 3:3). Jesus warned that "a man's enemies will be those of his own household" (Matthew 10:36). Guard against this by strengthening your family roots.

Elie Wiesel, a survivor of the Holocaust and winner of the 1986 Nobel Peace Prize, said, "The enemy is not love or hate, but indifference."

Don't let indifference keep you from passing on the importance of simple, but profound, family love. Water your roots.

2. Spiritual Roots

In a best-case scenario, spiritual roots will be closely intertwined with family roots.

I am proud of my Christian heritage. My family roots go deep into the soils of God's Word, the Church and Christianity. My relatives were on a first-name basis with the Maker of the universe. They called Him God, and He called me Betty. They taught me to talk to Him.

"Blood is thicker than water," says author Rees Howells, "but the Spirit is thicker than blood." As a tree leans, so shall it fall, unless a warm wind blows from the opposite direction. The influence of godly parents on their children is far greater than we will ever know this side of heaven.

Moses was adopted by King Pharoah's daughter, but he became the great leader chosen by God to take Israel out of Egypt's bondage. Why? Because his roots grew deep in his godly mother's teaching (see Exodus 2).

Timothy was influenced by two generations of godly parents (see 2 Timothy 1:5). Spiritual fitness must be promoted in the next generation or the flame will be extinguished. Deuteronomy 11:2 reminds us that we have to pass on the stories of our experiences with God because our children were not there to see them. They will have their own experiences if they walk with Him, but if we do not share ours, they will never know of God's influence over their roots.

Four-year-old, red-haired Ryan was attending a Kids' Krusade. "I'm looking for a kid who knows how to have fun," the crusade director told his audience of tots.

"Pick me, I'm lots of fun," called Ryan, jumping for joy. (The director picked him!) Ryan believes what his whole family tells him: "You are a wonderful boy. You have been chosen by God Himself. You are a priest of the King, you are holy and pure, you are God's very own." (See 1 Peter 2:9.)

We will believe what God says about us more readily if our parents believe it, too.

When parents drop the name *Jesus* frequently, faith is instilled in the next generation. Our friends Bob and Cheryl Watson got caught in a terrible storm during hurricane season. Sitting in their car outside Pizza Hut, they heard their daughter Brittany talking in the back seat.

"We can't hear you," they called to her over the pounding of the rain.

"I'm not talking to you," she yelled back. "I'm talking to God."

Parents have the opportunity to plant Gospel seed in the most fertile fields of all, the lives of their children, and then affirm with Scripture, "I have no greater joy than to hear that my children walk in truth" (3 John 4).

Lois Carnes, daughter of our friends Ed and Ruth Schlossmacher, wrote the following for the *Pentecostal Evangel*. Carl recommends it as a reading at the dedication of a baby:

Parents are responsible for the spiritual fitness of their children. Spiritual roots are best learned through experience rather than receiving information. Jesus Christ should be manifest in daily life, not just those areas that are church-related.

"Thou shalt love the Lord thy God with all thine heart, and thou shalt teach these words diligently unto thy children. Thou shalt talk of them when thou sittest in thine house, when thou walkest by the way, and when thou liest down, and when thou risest up" (Deuteronomy 6:5–7). We are experiencing an "information explosion." But we must teach our children the most important information, to worship and communicate with God by our example and modeling. The church cannot make the qualitative change in the lives of young people that can best be accomplished at home.

Two specific areas come to mind when I think about nurturing spiritual roots by teaching our children to worship and communicate with God. They are music and prayer.

MUSIC

I have never had lots of money. As the Perkins household of pastor's children, we did not have much, but we had love, security—and music. We grew up singing songs like "A Child of the King," "I Belong to the King" and "Now I Belong to Jesus." My dad was a happy man who woke up very early each morning whistling. He whistled while he worked, when he walked, while he drove. He taught us to whistle when we were very little.

My brother Don called from Indiana one time some years after we had both left home to live our own lives. During our twenty-minute conversation, it was evident he was depressed; life's circumstances had whittled away his smile.

We began to talk about our happy parents who survived parenting, pastoring, poverty and ill health but never lost their sense of humor or their love for music and singing. Don took his pulse, checked his roots. That was it! Don had pawned his saxophone to pay bills.

"Remember when you walked through the house," I asked him, "just a kid, playing fast music, jazz music? Do you remember sitting on the platform in a humble church in New Castle, Indiana, eyes closed, playing the old hymns and fast revival choruses? You were happy and you made other people, people who had come with their burdens, happy. Remember the old tune 'Revive Us Again'?"

Remembering our musical roots revived Don.

Music has special power when it is anointed in worshiping God. A few years back I met Sue Chrisco. Her songs at a beautiful retreat center where I was ministering made it easier than easy for me to speak. When I was asked recently to speak at the Hospital Christian Fellowship to be held at the Word of Life Christian Center in Hudson, Florida, I remembered Sue. She had written a song entitled "Dr. Jesus," about Jesus being needed to deliver a new baby into the faith. I thought it would be perfect for Sue to do a mini-concert at the conference and open with "Dr. Jesus."

But when I called Sue, I did not hear the lilt in her voice that I was expecting. Listening, I learned that because of the cares of life she had not been singing. We remembered the line from an old song, "Rescue the Perishing," that says, "Chords that were broken will vibrate once more." Feeders need to be fed, too, I reminded Sue. She decided to prepare a "music menu" to serve us at the conference. But since ministry is a two-way street, Sue was newly revitalized with fresh anointing even as she revived us.

Make music, and musical memories, part of the legacy of spiritual simplicity you pass on to your children.

PRAYER

Prayer works, and children need the secure legacy of knowing that it works. Our roots must go deep in the principles of prayer.

I once saw a book entitled *Birth Marks*. We tend to think of birth marks as bad, but what about good birth marks? My grandmothers, mother and I touched our abdomens while we carried our children and prayed for their development, health, safe deliveries and futures, quoting Isaiah 44:3: "I will pour My Spirit on your descendants, and My blessing on your offspring."

If you are carrying a baby, listen to this concept, which I call "Look, Speak and Hear":

> *Look.* Put a picture of a healthy baby in a convenient place where you can see it often. Fix in your mind the picture of your own beautiful child.
> *Speak.* Sing, whistle and pray for your unborn child.
> *Hear.* Listen to pleasant, happy music. Listen for natural sounds, the birds, the wind. And adopt Philippians 4:8: "Whatever things are true . . . noble . . . just . . . pure . . . lovely . . . [and] of good report . . . meditate on these things."

As you carry your child, you are creating the atmosphere of his or her environment. Just as surely as an improper diet and alcohol can harm your growing baby, so you can help him or her by what you feed your spirit.

My married daughter told me, "Mother, I love my daughter Erika so much that I can't help worrying that something might happen to her." I saw a poster that I had to buy: "Mirror, Mirror, on the Wall, I'm Like My Mother After All." Like her grandmother (my mother), and me, my daughter has to guard against worrying. Prayer is *not* worrying out loud!

"The people who receive anything from God that is rightfully theirs are the ones who hold fast to His promises . . . like a bulldog with a bone," says evangelist Lowell Lundstrom. He suggests five promises to hold fast to: "The Word of God, good things, godly traditions, our confidence and the professions of our faith."

Teach your children to pray, and pray for them, too. The Word promises, "Those that seek me early shall find me" (Proverbs 8:17, KJV). I believe that verse can be interpreted to mean seeking Him while we are at an early age, early each morning to start the day and early in a situation, before it gets out of hand.

Our dad taught us to pray, and we heard him pray. Mother and Dad prayed *with* us before we left for the day, and *for* us several times during the day. No small wonder I cannot even remember having a headache as a child. Not only that: I also had an abundance of self-confidence and security.

"To train a boy in the way he should go, you must go that way yourself," advised evangelist Billy Sunday. I would add that mentoring and modeling do not guarantee that a child will not wander some in his youth, so keep praying. In maturity he will return to his roots. Charles Stanley says that if a boy has a praying mother, he has to jump a whole bunch of hurdles to go to hell.

One final thought about spiritual roots: We need the Church. The Church belongs to Christ. It is our shelter in the time of storm, the cleft of the Rock to run into for shelter at the end of the week. Give me the Church: It is the most powerful instrument on earth.

I like mod cars and mod dress, but old-time religion is good enough for me. Jeremiah 6:16 tells us, "Stand in the ways and see, and ask for the old paths . . . and walk in [them]; then you will find rest for your souls." Sink your roots deeper into truth. Seek out the old paths, dig out the old wells.

3. Roots of Wisdom

What gems of wisdom do you recall learning from your parents? Check them against Scripture; weed out anything that smacks of stereotyping, bigotry or ignorance; then pass the remaining nuggets on to your children. It is all too easy for some of the old sayings to get lost.

My friend Kate Oaks sent me these:

> God will supply that which you have knee'd.
> Advice from an old optimist: Fall down six times, get up seven.
> Some people lay down their lives, trying to lay up money.
> Love at first sight is often cured by a second look.
> Arguments never settle things but prayer changes them.

When we Perkins children were little, Dad taught us, "God first." His wise words on marriage included, "When a child of God marries a child of the devil, he will have trouble with his father-in-law for the rest of his life." And to my brothers, "Don't be a louse; wait for your spouse." Our grandfather Dad Perky added great advice on husband (or wife) selection gleaned from his years as a builder: "Measure twice and you will only have to cut once."

Write down the words of wisdom you remember from your parents and grandparents, and sprinkle them into your own conversations with your family. Add your own, too; someday your sons and daughters will quote you and tell their children, "As your grandmother used to say. . . ."

4. Patriotism

I am a radical American. I am proud of my country. As I write it is only May, but I already have "Old Glory" waving from the top sundeck of our little stilt house here in Crystal Beach, in anticipation of the Fourth of July. I have already bought firecrackers, sparklers and a new pair of sweatpants. The left leg is blue and covered with stars; the right leg is all red and white stripes! I have made early plans for the 1996 Olympics in Atlanta, too: I already have my official U.S.A. Olympics T-shirt!

Our ancestors came to this country to establish a place of residence where freedom to worship was available to all. Later the founders of our nation guaranteed that right in the Constitution. Our coins declare it: "In God We Trust."

Thomas Jefferson served as president of the Washington, D.C., school board during his tenure as President of the United States. One of his duties on the board was to select the textbooks to be used by the students. He chose the Bible as the primary text with this rationale: "I have always said, and always will say, that the studious perusal of the sacred volume will make us better citizens" (from the *American Family Journal*).

In 1836 Truman and Smith published the *Eclectic First Reader* for William McGuffey, professor in Miami University, Oxford. My friend Shirley Moore from Belleville, Illinois, lent me one of her set to enjoy. The preface reads, "William Holmes McGuffey, outstanding educator and preacher, published a series of McGuffey readers. He combined both of these God-given talents in the preparation of these early textbooks."

Millions of copies were sold in their original, Christ-centered form. The character of our nation was molded in an upright manner through the repeated use of these textbooks over several generations.

In 1954 President Dwight D. Eisenhower signed a bill that added two words to the Pledge of Allegiance to the American flag: "under God."

Why do I say all this? Because I want to make the point that we need to pass on the simple truth about good, old-fashioned patriotism to the next generation. In order to do that, we need to understand the facts about our country's beginnings—facts that include God as a major player.

More than seventy years ago, on July 21, 1925, the "Monkey Trial" ended in Dayton, Tennessee. John T. Scopes was convicted of violating state law by teaching Darwin's theory of evolution. The conviction was later overturned, but it reveals a stark difference between then and now. Today it is the creationist who must stand trial while the evolutionist controls the gavel of educational law.

An optimist might note that if that much change could take place in less than seventy years, we could reverse current trends and bring about positive, revolutionary changes for our children and grandchildren. I would like to be an optimist about it; I hope we can make some changes. But I wonder why we even have to be fighting these battles when the intentions of our founding fathers are so clear in their writings. I am hurt when I hear people damning and slamming our nation. Let those people who do not want to live in a nation that believes in God change their citizenship to one of the many countries that do not have a Judeo-Christian heritage. You cannot have the perks without paying the price. And our children need to know that.

Start Again

What if you as a parent have made some bad calls, or created "bad roots" for your children?

When a golfer makes a bad shot and wants to redo it without adding an additional stroke to his score, he simply calls it a mulligan and starts again. You can do the same. Confess and repent. God will not change, but He changes things and circumstances.

I had no idea what Carl was doing downstairs with a spade and a rake one day until he came up and said to me, "Put your computer on pause. I have a surprise for you." As we walked down the steps he said, "Shut your eyes." He led me to a spot outside my writing studio door and said, "Open your eyes." He had planted a row of impatiens, plants that grow in vibrant colors.

"I feel sorry for you," he said, "coming and going in and out of that door, and all you see is a cement walk surrounded by dead pine needles."

Shortly afterward Carl was gone for several days speaking in Findlay, Ohio, and examining his roots in his first pastorate after he finished Bible school. While he was away I became so engrossed in writing that I forgot to water the impatiens. They became "impatient" for moisture, and one day I thought they were dead. Quickly I grabbed the sprinkler and soaked them well.

"He must not see them like this," I told myself. "He will think I don't appreciate his sacrifice, his love gift to me."

I fell into bed wearily that night. The next morning when I woke up and leaned way out over the balcony to see the impatiens, their roots and leaves had revived.

Roots can be revived. There may still be consequences for past mistakes, but if you have asked God's forgiveness for past sin, your relationship with God is restored, and you can start again to appreciate your heritage and make it an even better one to pass on to your offspring.

But what if you have "bad roots" to begin with? What if there seems to be nothing in your heritage of which to be proud, or what if some major flaw has dogged your family for generations?

If your mother or father or other relatives before them were alcoholics, learn from their mistakes, take preventive measures for yourself and your children and break the pattern. Reverse the curse! You might want to read Derek Prince's book about generational sin, *Blessing or Curse: You Can Choose* (Chosen, 1990) for help in doing just that. And remember that those relatives were made in the image of God, too. Try to discover something of value in their lives to tell your little ones.

I come from a long line of English men with a reputation for having strong opinions and making hard judgments. But God softens the roots if we are committed to walking with

Him. When my father died I realized he had left us a changed legacy: He never criticized others, did not scrutinize and judge my mother. Even when I blundered, he still believed in me and gave me his vote of confidence.

My brother Marvin has exhibited rigid roots that have made growth and self-expression difficult. He has a marvelous intellect and is a member of Mensa and Intertel, so he is not easily swayed by foolishness, and particularly by his sister's foolishness.

But a big man can afford to be magnanimous. He once sent me a mug with his picture on it that said, "Every time I try to see things your way I get a headache." Last Christmas time I received a letter from him that said, "I have been reading a men's magazine called *New Man*. That's what I want for my wife, Sharon, for Christmas—a new man. And that's what I want, too. We're both sick of the old one." He was serious, and saw need for a change. It takes strength to admit need.

It is never too late to change, to start again. A friend of ours named Wendell had two boys who told me, "We feel that if praying and going to church were important, Dad would do it." He didn't. But when a new baby arrived in the family, something changed. The family took her to church, dedicated her to the Lord and dedicated themselves to having family devotions together. And they have followed through.

You, too, can start again. Get serious, guard your roots and water them with the refreshing rain of the Holy Spirit, so they do not dry up and cause your children to despair of life. Our sins will be visited down to the third and fourth generations, the Bible tells us (see Exodus 20:5). But speak God's grace and the mercy of Christ to your children if you have exposed some bad roots. You, too, can ask God to forgive, revive, soften and strengthen your roots.

What Do We Have to Offer?

Remember when dads, mothers, schoolteachers, Presidents and doctors were almost universally considered worthy of awe and wonder? They portrayed high moral standards and were loyal to the truth, straight as arrows. Remember when priests, rabbis and pastors were shepherds, not celebrities? They carried no big sticks, but had big hearts, and saw character as more important than accomplishments.

I believe the Holy Spirit is moving upon the earth again as in simple faith, people are praying. The wind of prayer has moved the heart and hand of God.

I took down the following lines from a poem during a sermon one Sunday:

> Children see us as we are, not a distant star.
> In their eyes there's no pretending.
> Their lives are waiting to discern
> All that they can learn from us,
> And Whom we trust in.

Look into the mirror. Are you becoming a person of simplicity? Will you have roots of simplicity to pass on to your children? All we have to offer is the legacy we leave behind.

ᒥᕮᴎ

Grow Old, Grow Up,
but Stay Childlike

A s we explore the virtues of childlike simplicity, we have to face the simple fact that we will grow old. We have no choice in the matter. A person is physically youthful only once, but can by choice remain immature forever. Will we choose to grow *up* in the process of growing old? Beautiful babies and young people are results of nature, but beautiful old people are works of art.

In this chapter we will laugh at the old clichéd concept of second childhood and have some fun at the expense of the senior cits (labeled "Q-tips" here in the retirement state of Florida!). Then we will learn together about developing unto, and into, childlike Christian maturity.

Grow Old . . .

One day as Carl and I were in the van running an errand, we turned the corner off Alternate 19 onto Drew Street.

Suddenly Carl slammed on his brakes. Cars behind us did the same, like dominoes.

A tiny, bent crone had stumbled off the curb and fallen, flinging her brown paper bag of fresh apples into the street, where they were rolling in the grit like bowling balls. I jumped out and lifted her to her feet. Tears ran down her creased old cheeks as she asked hoarsely, "Is this what 'old' means?" It broke my heart.

As I picked up her apples and walked her into the security of her retirement complex entrance, she told me, "I'm in pretty good shape. As long as I don't get down, I do O.K. Thanks for helping me get up."

Yes, "old" means having your body give out, having it betray you and refuse to perform as it did when you were younger. That famous genius author "Unknown" voiced what must be a universal wish among oldsters:

> When my form is bent with age and gets to looking
>   shoddy,
> How nice 'twould be to trade it in, and get a brand-new
>   body.

My husband has written a book entitled *If You're Over the Hill, You Oughta Be Goin' Faster*. In serious discussion about this chapter of *Simplicity*, he shouted, "I despise aging. I refuse to get old."

"You only have one alternative," I reminded him. "Death."

"I prefer that," he shot back.

Carl has argued with God and with nature over this subject for the past ten years. He is a remarkable 74-year-old man with something always cooking on the back burner. This scorches me sometimes! Carl has a stereo mind. The man is continually looking for a greater challenge and higher mountain to climb. After his last physical examination, the doctor informed us, "Carl's heart and lungs are 35 years old."

Some seniors are not so fortunate. That same doctor examined our neighbor Cliff and asked him, "How do you feel when you get up in the morning?"

"Amazed!" admitted Cliff.

Still, Carl and I are growing old. We had pictures taken on our last anniversary with our relatives Earl and Pearl Rodgers, and we have the evidence to prove that our faces have cheated neither the calendar nor Father Time.

On the national bulletin board (our refrigerator), we have posted this gem clipped from a newsletter:

> My face in the mirror isn't wrinkled or drawn.
> My furniture is dusted; the cobwebs are gone.
> My garden is lovely, and so is my lawn.
> I don't think I will ever put my glasses back on!

Our friendly geriatrician, Dr. Fred Roever, has compiled enough "geriatric banter" to produce his own mirth book. Here are some from our collection:

Yes, I'm religious. I do believe in the "hereafter." Every time I go into another room, I ask myself, What did I come in here after?

When Myrtle babysits her grandchildren, she keeps getting their Pampers mixed up with her Depends.

At your 25th class reunion, you wear a nametag so your classmates can remember who you are. At your 50th reunion, you wear a nametag so *you* can remember who you are.

You can live to be a hundred if you give up all the things that make you want to live to be a hundred.

Bumper sticker for the hypochondriac: "I'd rather be ailing."

And Carl and I love the following poem we found somewhere:

When I Am Old

I'll live with my children, and bring them great joy,
To repay all I've had from each girl and boy.
I shall draw on the walls and scuff up the floor;
Run in and out without closing the door.
I'll hide frogs in the pantry, socks under my bed.
Whenever they scold me, I'll just hang my head.

I'll run and I'll romp, always fritter away
The time to be spent doing chores every day.
I'll pester my children when they're on the phone.
When they're busy, I won't leave them alone.
Hide candy in the closets, rocks in my drawer,
Never pick up my clothes, but leave them on the floor.

Dash off to the park and not wash a dish,
I'll plead for allowance whenever I wish.
I'll stuff up the plumbing and deluge the floor.
As soon as they've mopped it, I'll flood it some more.
When they correct me, I'll lie down and cry.
Kicking and screaming, not a tear in my eye.

I'll take all their pencils and flashlights, and then,
When they buy new ones, I'll take them again.
I'll spill glasses of milk to complicate each meal,
Eat my bananas and just drop the peel.
Put toys on the table, spill jam on the floor,
I'll break lots of dishes as though I were four.

What fun I shall have, what joy it will be,
To live with my children as they lived with me!

Author Unknown

The critics warned America that a movie star would make a poor President. I refuse to debate politics or religious labels in my books, but you have to admit that Ronald Reagan had the ability to chuckle at his aging process. I would say he increased the "mirth rate" dramatically while he was in office. He told many good stories, but this classic, which I read in one of his speeches, has long been my favorite:

An elderly couple had just started to put on their pajamas when she got a yen for ice cream.

"I'll go buy some," he said.

"Oh," she said, "you're a dear. I want vanilla with fudge topping. Write it down, or you'll forget."

"I won't forget," he assured her.

"With some whipped cream on top," she added.

"Vanilla with fudge topping, whipped cream on top," he recited.

"And a cherry, too."

"And a cherry, too," he repeated.

"Please write it down," she pleaded. "You won't remember."

"I won't forget," he insisted. "Vanilla ice cream, fudge topping, whipped cream, cherry on top. I won't forget; I don't need to write it down."

It took the old husband so long that by the time he returned, she was sound asleep. He woke her up and handed her the paper bag containing her snack. When she opened it, she discovered a ham sandwich.

"I told you to write it down," she said after she unwrapped it. "You forgot the mustard!"

One more poem, this one clipped from Barbara Johnson's Spatula Ministry newsletter:

A Retiree's Lament

Thought I'd let my doctor check me, 'cause I didn't
    feel quite right.
All those aches and pains annoyed me, and I couldn't
    sleep at night.

He could find no real disorder, but he wouldn't let it rest,
What with Medicare and Blue Cross, it wouldn't hurt to test.
To the hospital he sent me, though I didn't feel that bad.
He arranged for them to give me every test that could be
    had.
I was fluoroscoped, cystoscoped, my aging frame displayed.
Stripped upon an ice-cold table, while my gizzards were
    x-rayed.
I was checked for worms and parasites, for fungus and the
    crud,
While they pierced me with long needles, taking samples of
    my blood.

Doctors came to check me over, probed and pushed and
    poked around.
And to make sure I was living, they wired me up for sound.
They have finally concluded (their results have filled a
    page),
What I have, will someday kill me: My affliction is old age!

There are enough "old," "senile" and "Alzheimer's" jokes
to fill more than eleven chapters of more than one book,
and it is best that we laugh at age and at ourselves before
others have a chance to laugh at us. Then we can get on
with living.

Grow Up . . .

We have talked a lot about growing old; now let's talk
about growing up.

I could write three books on creative aging just by hanging around the Post Office near our house. Oldsters love
getting mail. Many of them go to the Post Office several
times in one day. You know that your life has become simplified when a trip to the Post Office is the highlight of your
day, every day.

Two men, gray and bent, Mr. Harvey using a walker, and Mr. Bertram poking along with his cane, blocked the Post Office doorway. From the lobby I heard Mr. Harvey say to Mr. Bertram, "Well, I gotta go."

"What you gotta go home for?" asked Mr. Bertram.

"I gotta go home and worry."

"What will you worry about?" asked Mr. Bertram.

"I dunno," said Mr. Harvey, "but I'll think of something."

As they continued to make their exit, a pretty, young chick from Pointe Seaside parked her Mercedes and rushed toward the door. Trying to be friendly in spite of the fact that their slow, careful egress was holding her up, she smiled and said to the two old gents, "Have a nice day!"

"Don't tell me what kind of day to have," Mr. Harvey responded with a furrowed brow. "I'm tired of being told what to do, of people shovin' me around."

Inside, the woman sighed as she inserted her key into her mailbox.

"What ails him?" she asked me. Before I could answer, we realized that Mr. Bertram had lingered.

"I'll tell you what's ailing him," he replied. "He's got hemorrhoids, his daughter never writes or calls and his overweight wife nags him."

"How do you know these things?" the woman asked.

Mr. Bertram winked. "I didn't come in on the last turnip truck. Hang around 82 more years, darlin', and you'll jist know." Mr. Bertram is growing old—and growing up.

Not all Q-tips are as edgy as Mr. Harvey was that day, and many of them are growing up with grace and style. Charlie McMahan was hit with last year's hideous hurricane. His pretty little condo on the boat channel was flooded, a mess. We asked him how he fared, what he did to cope.

"I prayed to God for safety, called a friend, went on a Caribbean cruise, then cleaned up the mess two weeks later," he told us.

Charlie's birth certificate proves he is 87, but he has fooled a lot of people with his ability to soar above his circumstances. He spends time in prayer each morning and reads his Bible every day. "If you return to the Almighty, you will be built up" (Job 22:23). People twenty years his junior (mostly women!) think he is their age.

Joan Rivers has a knack of inserting her famous "Grow up!" into an interview when she dislikes a person or disagrees with his or her viewpoint. If only it were that easy!

Growing up is a two-way street involving a happy medium between the ability to be happy yourself and the ability to make others happy. Warren Wiersbe has said, "The mind grows as it takes in; the heart grows as it gives out."

Carl visited the old home church recently where my grandparents grew up in God. My Aunt Shirley still plays the organ there, and Aunt Gertrude still plays the piano. Both of them assist in a radio broadcast. They minister mirth and music in nursing home and jail services. They must agree with Henry Martyn's comment: "If [God] has work for me to do, I cannot die."

"I pray that you may prosper," John the apostle said, "and be in health, just as your soul prospers" (3 John 2). We are considered lambs, but God's will is that we grow up and develop into sheep who serve God and in turn serve other lambs.

I led a women's retreat at Capital Christian Center in Sacramento, California. While I was there I heard the Rev. Glen Cole, pastor of the Center, suggest that to grow up in Christ, we must "reach the unreached, teach the reached and then train and motivate the reached to start the cycle again."

That confirms my thoughts about roots in the last chapter. One of the rewards of growing older is seeing the growth progress of your children and grandchildren. You have to work to put down roots, grow up, and then put down roots again—for your descendants. It is work, but it works and brings satisfaction.

I got a letter from our friend Pennie Kloos. She told about one night when she came home dead tired from a busy Sunday to find that Ricky, one of her four little boys, wanted to talk.

"Is Jesus in my heart?" he asked.

"Only if you asked Him to come in," Pennie explained.

Without hesitation he prayed, "Jesus, come in my heart right now."

That was wonderful enough, but a day or two later Pennie's pastor husband, Rick, was playing ball with the church league and slid home, skinning his knee. Little Ricky hurried to the bathroom with his dad, applied peroxide and prayed, "Jesus, take away the pain in my daddy's knee right now."

"Train up a child in the way he should go, and when he is old [and sometimes when he is not so old] he will not depart from it" (Proverbs 22:6). But little Ricky's conversion might not have happened if his mother had been too immature to put aside her own fatigue to "reach the unreached."

I want to draw a contrast. I know of a heartbreaking situation in a nearby state where a fourteen-year-old girl lies awake at night all alone, afraid, worrying about her mother, who is out with her boyfriend. Her mother is growing old, but not up.

Growing up may require you to play second fiddle, to be a door-opener, to exercise the ministry of helps. In a symphony orchestra the first violin would never sound so sweet were it not for the harmony of the second fiddle. You may be overqualified for a job, an assistant to a person inferior to you in age and experience, but when you work, shine your maturity.

"Humble yourself [grow up] under the mighty hand of God, that he may exalt you in due time" (1 Peter 5:6). The most essential people I know are bridges. "I sought for a man [to] stand in the gap," says Ezekiel 22:30. Harry Emerson Fosdick said, "No horse gets anywhere until he is harnessed. Steam and gas drive things after they are confined. No Niagara is ever turned into light and power until it is tunneled. No life is usable until it is focused, mature and disciplined."

Grow up. Invest in people. A plaque in the foyer of Methodist Hospital in Houston, Texas, reads:

> I stand by the side of a current that's deeper
>   far than the sea.
> And storm-beaten crafts of every draught
>   come in to be healed by me.
> But some have more sin than fever, and some have
>   more grief than pain.
> God help me make whole, both body and soul,
>   before they go out again.

Another aspect of growing up: During the General Council of the Assemblies of God in Minneapolis, I heard speaker Charles Crabtree comment on Jeremiah 50:11: "You have grown fat." He cautioned that the immature person seeks to be blessed instead of grounded, and that we should beware lest the thrill of the miraculous become more exciting than the development of character. We believe in the supernatural, but there is a temptation to glorify the works of God at the expense of growing up in the life of God.

Grow up. God has not promised us an easy journey, but a safe one. Christianity can be condensed into four words: admit, submit, commit and transmit. There are no drafted men or women in the army of God because God knows volunteers make the best soldiers. I know a lot of talkers who are not walkers. The uniform does not make the fighter. A mule in a tuxedo will still make a public donkey of himself.

"Let us live as people who are prepared to die, and die as people who are prepared to live forever," urged James S. Stewart. Grow up. In the spiritual battle of life, God needs front-line warriors who are fearless. Fight the enemy. If your faith did not make you a stranger in this wicked world, the devil's hounds would not bark at you.

Paul said that we are to grow up into Him in all things. His will is to give us grace, to give gifts, to perfect us, to give us unity, faith and knowledge, that we should mature by speaking the truth and be measured by the stature of Christ (see Ephesians 4:7–15).

Life Goes On

For the Christian, life literally does go on—forever. The Scriptures remind us, "If in this life only we have hope in Christ, we are of all men the most pitiable" (1 Corinthians 15:19). Dale Nelson sang a great song called "I'm Goin' to a City" at the funeral of my first husband's mother, Dorothy (Mamaw) Upchurch, not long ago.

It could not have been more appropriate. Mamaw was 94 when she died. She had been preceded in death by her son (my first husband) many years ago.

The day before she died, my orchid tree was in full bloom, so I took a blossom and stopped by the nursing home to see her. She opened her eyes just long enough to look at me and say, "Greater is he that is in you, than he that is in the world" (1 John 4:4, KJV). I thought she was just mumbling to herself. Now I realize that was her last will and testament, her personal instructions to me. Since her death I have run into some obstacles, but each time I look at the little pink-striped jewelry box that her daughter Helen gave me to remind me of Mamaw, I am spurred on to make it by the admonition of her last words.

One Sunday night following a message on foreign missions, I was hurrying down the aisle when I felt a hand pat
my lower back. I could not believe my eyes: It was Daphne
Brann, nearly 105 years old. Why would a woman that old
be out at night and interested in missionary ministry? I
remarked on how unbelievably vibrant she was.

Her only reply as she grinned was, "Betty, 'The grass with-
ers, the flower fadeth, but he that doeth the will of God, and
the Word of God, endureth forever'" (paraphrase of Isaiah
40:8). Daphne Brann is 106 now, still going and still growing. She is an enduring woman on her way to an eternal city.

. . . But Stay Childlike

Too many people grow old, grow up and then allow themselves to become *childish*. I know we cannot always control the effects of aging that play tricks on our minds and
emotions, but if we are serious about aging gracefully, we
will remember to build the *childlike* qualities Jesus prized
for His followers into our old age. When people of lesser
age describe us as "young at heart," it is not only a supreme
compliment about our attitude, but a "job well done!" in
terms of our spiritual growing-up process.

If you think the conclusion of this book will just be a
place for the etc., P.S. and "Oh, by the way" leftovers, a place
where I will put the things that did not fit into the ten previous chapters, you are right. If you did not have time to
read the entire book but can spare ten minutes, read on for
the conclusion.

ELEVEN

Let Simplicity
Be Your Motto

Writing this book on simplicity for the past fifteen months has been one of the most complicated struggles of my entire life. I have felt "swamped." We use that word without knowing its origin and meaning, but if you have ever visited Florida's cypress swamp at midnight and seen and felt the hopeless despair of that blackness, you know what I mean by "swamped."

On one particular day during the writing of this book, I was typing hard and fast, enjoying my writing and trucking right along. I thought I would meet my manuscript deadline easily. Then Ma Bell allowed eight phone calls to come, throwing a monkey wrench into my organized simplicity. And it was not even noon yet! I pretended to pull my hair and complained out loud.

"Go to the beach for an hour and put that dumb phone on silent record," said Carl. "What you don't know can't hurt you. That's why we bought that kind of phone, so let it help you."

"It's not that simple!" I retorted loudly.

"No," he replied quietly, "it's not that complicated. That's why we got the answering machine. Let it do its work. You can return the calls tonight."

So I took a bag of stale cookies and a bottle of lemonade and retreated to quiet simplicity. Leaving the crowded part of the beach, I walked slowly, leaving a trail of broken, stale cookies behind me. It was such fun playing Pied Piper: Hundreds of seagulls followed me. I started throwing small bits into the air for them to catch.

One young gull flew into the crowded competition. I aimed toward him, but bigger birds bumped him and stole his treat. A soft feather fell from his young coat and stuck to the Tropic Tan oil on the top of my left foot.

I almost cried. But suddenly I realized that if God's eye is on the sparrow, He would replace the feather for that baby gull. I brought the feather home and put it in a tiny bud vase in the kitchen window. Each time I look at its simplicity, I can almost hear God say, "I have his small need in focus, and yours. Trust Me."

Having emerged now from the blackness and discouragement of my months-long swamp, I have found several simple keys to survival that can help us recapture the beauty of childlike simplicity in our lives. Let me list some you are aware of, and then focus in on some less familiar ones.

Through Moses, God gave us the Ten Commandments, keys to survival and simplicity. Read them. They still apply.

The sweet singer, King David, through trial and error, sinning and repentance, found some keys that gave him a second chance: God's grace, mercy and forgiveness.

Through Jesus, our finest example, God gave us two keys that summarize the Ten Commandments. They are (1) love God and (2) love people.

But it is Solomon, a son produced out of one of David's greatest sins, and a man acclaimed as the wisest person who ever lived, to whom I want us to listen in this last chapter.

If experience is the best teacher, Solomon deserves our attention. He had palaces, fountains, gold, servants, chariots, armies, too many wives and too many concubines. After all his experimenting, Solomon handed down three simple keys to survival and penned a book of down-to-earth instruction that anyone who can read can use.

Solomon's Simple Keys to Survival

Most of us are familiar with the Ten Commandments, with David's story and with Jesus' two, marvelously concise instructions. But few of us read Solomon's writings regularly, and particularly not the book of Ecclesiastes. I want to share with you what I have learned from this man who asked God for wisdom.

Solomon, having lived a long, adventurous (and not always righteous) life, said that "the conclusion of the whole matter" about living a simple, satisfying and productive life rests on three simple actions. He did not offer a series of tapes, videos and books or any expensive seminars or conferences. He gave this advice: Love God, love your own wife and enjoy your food. He offered three additional pieces of advice. They are:

1. Obey the rules (Ecclesiastes 9:9; 12:13).
2. Work hard (Ecclesiastes 2:24; 3:13, 22; 5:18, 19; 9:10).
3. Trust God (Ecclesiastes 2:24–26; 5:1, 4; 7:18; 12:13–14).

Let's look at each of Solomon's three pieces of advice in turn.

1. Obey the Rules

"Enjoy life" (9:9). "Keep His commandments" (12:13). Solomon tells us that obeying the rules, even if they sometimes seem out of whack with society or common sense, is important.

A few years ago Lou Whitaker of the Detroit Tigers baseball team stepped up to the plate and hit the ball over the fence and out of the park. It was a home run, there was no doubt about it, yet Lou Whitaker, like every baseball player who hits a homer, ran all the bases. Why? It is the rule.

Jesus died at Calvary to pay for our passport to heaven. There is no doubt He has given us free passage, but we must obey the rule and run the bases of life. The Betty Malz version of 1 Corinthians 13:11 reads, "When I was a child, I thought as a child, but when I became a man, I put away childish things and began playing the game by The Rules."

Samson went from hero to zero because he ignored the rules. Evaluate his fix. Being famous, handsome, successful, wealthy and strong does not exempt us from the rules, and it did not exempt Samson. In our lives there are the "and suddenlies," the tornadoes of the unexpected that happen. But Samson knew he had created his own crisis. He slipped into the camp of the nation that was at war with his own country. His head was not in a "noose" until he deliberately put it into the lap of a pretty pagan woman. Her people captured him. Her people poked out his eyes with hot branding irons.

Now blind, the still-strong, still-famous Samson was forced to walk in circles, chained to a grist mill, grinding grain alongside mules who did the same work he did.

Our pastor, Steve Lambert, mapped Samson's four steps back. Good things are expensive, but Samson went from zero to hero again.

First, Samson had to admit his failure. He had created his own problem by disobeying the rules God had given him, so he took the blame and total responsibility for it, asking God to help him avenge his enemy.

There is a lesson here for us. If life is not as good as it once was for you, look inside. Have you disobeyed the rules?

Second, Samson did not give up. He realized his moment of opportunity and plotted his course back. He knew it would be expensive to get his strength back. He would get a little lad to lead him to the pillars of the temple where the enemy army was celebrating his loss and their victory. He would fell that building and kill more people by his death than in his life. What a sad truth! He could have accomplished this same victory with his eyes intact had he just obeyed the rules.

Third, since Samson had lost his eyes he had to admit his complete dependence on God. "I need You. I am without strength."

Fourth, Samson did not *win* the victory; he *paid* a costly price for it. He died under the ruins. A victory that involved his own death was an expensive one.

If you are in a fix, listen to Solomon's advice. Simply turn about-face and obey the rules while you still have eyes to see clearly. God can change circumstances for you if you admit your need and take the opportunities He makes available.

2. Work Hard

Solomon admonished us to work hard (9:10) and to enjoy the work of our hands (2:24; 3:22). It is not a sin to rest; even God rested after He had created for six days. But it is a sin to be lazy. Don't expect a stranger to wipe your nose. Sometimes we have to grab ourselves by the back of the neck, pick ourselves up by our own bootstraps, encourage ourselves *in the Lord* and work out our own salvation with fear and trembling (Philippians 2:12). Sometimes we have to say to ourselves, "Just *do* it."

Take hold of your relationship problem, your weight problem, your dilemma at work. Many times people say, "Help!" when they really mean, "Do it for me." Jeremiah 33:3 tells us to "dial direct" when we cannot do things on our own: "Call unto me, and I will answer thee, and show thee great and mighty things, which thou knowest not" (KJV).

Do not let criticism hinder your work. I wish I could remember who said "Don't let the moral midgets slap you down." I say that to myself and apply it frequently. And Ben Haden says, "It's not what is said about you the day you die, but what can be said about your ambition for your work every day you live, that really counts."

Know your limitations, then do your best. If you cannot swim, wade. Be content with your work. Sometimes the biggest apple has the biggest worm.

Many times you cannot fix your situation, cannot alter your church, repair your car or change your job. You cannot ride a dead horse. Remove the saddle and go on to another horse (project). Some relationships cannot be resolved. Some broken things cannot be repaired. Avoid the hassle factor. The simplest way may be to change jobs, change churches, change cars. We cannot keep chasing our kids, working to please them. Pray, and let them return.

Ask God for a workable situation. Then work hard to do your part and enjoy your work.

3. Trust God

Worship, obey and trust God. "I know not the way He leads, but I know my Guide. What have I to fear?" asked Martin Luther. What, indeed?

"Children, obey your parents" (Ephesians 6:1) is a Scripture with a promise. God is our Father, and Solomon suggests that we must honor (worship), obey and trust Him (7:18; 12:1, 13). It is possible to obey without honoring, but it is not possible to honor Him without obeying Him. When we do obey and honor, we are the winners.

Self-confidence is helpful, but self-help sometimes is no help at all. The self-sacrifice that comes with trusting God is the real way to find yourself. You get everything when you lose yourself and find Him. Don't be in such a hurry to go into business for yourself, spiritually speaking. When you deny yourself, obey and trust God, you qualify to reign with Him. Then, not now, you will get everything that is coming to you (see Matthew 16:12–28).

Karen Holland is the producer and host of "Miracles in America," a local cable broadcast. She puts trusting God this way: "Kids used to sing the silly little song, 'My dad's bigger than your dad.' God is our Father (Mark 14:36). As simple children we can cast all our cares upon Him for He cares for His children (1 Peter 5:7). This is clear: You are a very special child of a very special Father. The Word will come through for you."

You can trust Him; He will fight for you:

> The tools of our trade aren't for marketing or manipulation, but they are for demolishing . . . corrupt culture. [They are] powerful God-tools for smashing warped philosophies, tearing down barriers erected against the truth of God. . . . [These] tools are ready at hand for clearing the ground of every obstruction and building lives of obedience into maturity.
>
> 2 Corinthians 10:4, TM

Obey and trust God. "There remains therefore a rest for the people of God" (Hebrews 4:9). Rest in, lean back on, your Lord.

Several years ago Catherine Marshall summed it up in her own words when she said, "I suffered jangled nerves: too much mail, too much publicity, too many meetings, too much television, too many newspapers, articles and self-help books to read. We read too much. We cannot, must not close our eyes to the present and future, but we are overly informed. One morning the Holy Spirit impressed me, 'Read nothing but the Bible for three months.' It healed me."

This is the simple pattern that Solomon offers us: Obey the rules, work hard and trust God.

Summing Up Simplicity

I told you this chapter would contain all the ideas I just could not fit in anywhere else, as I try to sum up simplicity in simple terms. Here goes.

1. *We must eliminate and prioritize.* The enemies of our simplicity and tranquillity are the intrusions of life. We must let our quiet be deliberate.

The Malz answering machine has this message: "In order to avoid solicitors, we are asking you to leave your name and phone number. We will either lift up or call you right back. When you hear the beep, you will have only eighteen short seconds to leave your message. Thank you much." This has eliminated long hours on the phone and simplified our lives.

2. *Tune up with God.* Early on March 23, 1995, just at sunrise, I listened carefully. I heard a mockingbird. She was consistent and sang four times the same melody. It sounded like "Easter, Easter, Easter, Easter."

What a simple, yet profound, hope! Synchronize yourself early each morning with God. Take the long-range look. Will what is troubling me today matter five years from now? Is it going to affect people or things? Keep in mind what our friend Jerry Dickman suggested—that our real core values revolve around our families. People. Is what is consuming you temporary, or does it have spiritual or eternal value? Don't sweat the small stuff and get stuck in the sand dunes of the immediate.

3. *Delegate.* You cannot do it all. Ask for help. Admit you are tired and just cannot handle one more thing.

4. *Plan to make one trip do it all.* I shop for groceries only once every two weeks to conserve time. I try to park

a distance from the store so I can walk in the sun and exercise on my way to and from the car. We need God's vitamin C, His solar energy. You can get it this way in small doses.

5. *Unscramble and declutter.* Get rid of that car phone so you can drive to church in reflective silence. Unplug your phone during dinner so you can enjoy your food and family uninterrupted. Make a list each morning, numbering the things that must be done according to their importance. If the insignificant ones do not get done, no big loss. You have accomplished the more important. Time is too short to get sidetracked, to major in trivia.

When I played women's basketball in high school, our coach, Tex Black, had a time rule. When we had only ten minutes left, he would call, "Time out," and whisper, "No more risks. Play deliberately."

Play deliberately. Jesus is coming soon. The devil is our opponent in this life-and-death game. He knows we are too informed to lose the game to the obvious flaws, but will rob us instead of our simplicity in Christ, our lifeline.

"Cast all your care upon Him, for He cares for you" (1 Peter 5:7). You can simplify your life by rolling your burdens on Him, the One upon whose shoulder government will be, the One who is in control of the nations.

Let simplicity be your motto. He will help you, if you let Him have His way.